AF478145

# Articulating Gender, Narrating the Nation:
## Allegorical Femininity in Romanian Fiction

*Ileana Alexandra Orlich*

EAST EUROPEAN MONOGRAPHS, BOULDER
DISTRIBUTED BY COLUMBIA UNIVERSITY PRESS, NEW YORK
2004

# Contents

# Illustrations

The putting into discourse of "woman" as that process diag-
nosed in France as intrinsic to the condition of modernity;
[is] indeed, the valorization of the feminine, woman, and her
obligatory...historical connotations, as somehow intrinsic to
new and necessary modes of thinking, writing, speaking.

Alice Jardine
*Gynesis: Configurations of
Women and Modernity*

But what if the object began to speak?

Luce Irigaray
*Speculum of Other Woman*

# Introduction

This book maps the role of women in shaping the modern Romanian nation by examining how Romanian literature and culture have been aligned with the feminine presence. My primary interest is to argue convincingly for the valorization of the feminine marginalized or unremarked in a Romanian mainstream literary theory traditionally filled with a patriarchal mode of seeing and being in the world.

While I consider literature to be a cultural ensemble on an equal level of supremacy with the nation and a space where new borders between historical consciousness and reality are negotiated, I argue that (1) the interest in female figures in Romanian literature parallels the rise and prominence of the Romanian nation in the late nineteenth- and early twentieth-centuries; and (2) the emphasis on femininity, as an aesthetic and cultural category deeply rooted in the sociopolitical life of the nation, is as political as it is aesthetic. At the dawn of what is generally considered modern Romania, a period that covers the 1890s to the 1930s, the disciplining of various social classes, the changing rural environment and the emergence of urban areas, the rise of consumerism, and the invention of humdrum routine in the cities, have all brought to the fore women's essential role in shaping the culture and the need to broaden the cultural frame with which to understand Romania's modern society.

The five works I have identified as interpretive readings for this volume reveal the extent to which the modern Romania nation cannot be understood without proper emphasis on and ample reference to the textualization of femininity in a culture traditionally marked as masculine and patriarchal. My goal in each of the book's five free-standing essays is to examine the extent to which the master discourse of Romanian literature since the late nineteenth century had to mirror a new space and articulate new voices that refused to stay silent in its sphere of fictional representation.[1]

What is necessary before one can hope to understand the modern Romanian nation is to dismantle the patriarchal frame of male boundaries and to unravel the feminine spaces of culture that, as Julia Kristeva has pointed out, have always connoted the female.[2] As I trace the emergence and highlight the permanence of femininity and of feminine spaces overshadowed by the facades of masculinity, my approach is to pay particular attention to the portrayal and function of women protagonists and the degree to which their lives and roles on the domestic or public front can be disentangled from the fabric of the nation.

While the relation between women's voices and national identity is far too complex to be fully analyzed in this volume, it is important to mention that, as Julia Kristeva has pointed out in a different context, by 1929, a time when several of the works discussed in this volume had been published, those pillars that had traditionally supported the concept of a nation – economic homogeneity, historical tradition, and linguistic unity – had been endlessly rearranged.[3] But while the concrete links between the rise of women's voices and the large conceptual changes that called for the emphasis on national identity in Romania remain to be historically documented, at the very least it is clear that in the late nineteenth and early twentieth centuries, women were put into discursive circulation in significant, new ways.

As multiple voices that animated everyday life, the feminine protagonists discussed in the following chapters reverberate in quite different tones from the silent voices of the subaltern gender of the traditionally male-dominant discourse that has obscured or rendered invisible women's cultural identities. Turned into allegories that alter the critical landscape of Romania's literary critical tradition, these female characters become, in Walter Benjamin's words, a "revelatory instrument,"[4] which at once mimes the visual image and releases what Terry Eagleton calls "a fresh polyvalence of meaning"[5] transforming once integral meanings into startling new ways. As allegorical signifiers that cannot be grasped through the visual image alone, the newly recognized literary interpretations of female characters inscribe their own network of affinities across the space of Romanian history and produce new inflections in their own representation as emblematic figures reinforced in iconographic terms in the representative narratives of the nation. My examination of these feminine portraits, which are woven into the invisible, inner structure of the fictional works discussed here, requires a break with conventional criticism, as I seek to read deeper into their literary representations and bring them into an illuminating correspondence with the nation.

In the 1880s, for example, the novel *Mara* recasts historical tradition and linguistic unity as powerful fictional determinants in fashioning the country's national prominence. As an allegorical presence, the protagonist Mara, who substantiates her ethnic identity by her stubborn practice of Orthodox Christian faith, defines the cultural and religious memory of the Romanian community striving for continuity in the province of Banat in central western Romania, an area long disputed between Catholic Austro-Hungarians and Orthodox Romanians. At Ancuța's Inn (*Tales from Ancuța's Inn*), the confluence of cultural memory produces an ideal of community held together by symbolic common denominators that human groupings, united in the space of a fictional inn and its allegorically-constructed women innkeepers, embrace as nation. In *The Hatchet* the domain of the agricultural economy and of the human relationships developed through sheepherding and sustained through women's work on the domestic front is representative of a sociocultural ensemble that possesses a solidity rooted in another corresponding cultural ensemble – an age-old ballad that fulfills a double function: it substantiates the territorial and cultural continuity of the shepherd population acting as symbolic denominator of all Romanian communities, no matter how divided politically or geographically; and it reactivates the discourse of the past into the present precisely to call continuity into question, challenge, and ultimately disrupt the master narrative of the ballad that debased the struggles of women and domesticated their resistance to patriarchal order.

A novel like Hortensia Papadat-Bengescu's *The Disheveled Maidens* (1926) brings up the sexual, cultural, and social emancipation of women whose voices and newly appropriated townswoman spaces open to unassimilated otherness are inextricably linked to the rise of an urban culture within a modern, economically homogenized Romania. The feminine observer's interest in Bucharest, the country's capital, illuminates the relations between modernity and urbanization and elaborates on the city's cultural spaces and overlapping human interactions as inscriptions of her own consciousness. Even when they are left out of the community's sociosymbolic structure, women are the écriture of the text by becoming identified with the allegorical image that invests the text with the sacrificial aspect ingrained in Romania's sociocultural set of religious tradition and Christian beliefs. In spite of her social marginality, the protagonist of *Fefeleaga*, for example, is placed at the center of a sociohistorical context, which is that of the Romanian Orthodox civilization and its laical ramifications, where she appears as the closest approximation to an exemplar of Christian redemption achieved through suffering.

Thus the Romanian nation finds itself reflected in the fictional constructs of novels through the intercession of women speaking as subjects and acting with knowledge and authority as subjects imagined not only in female, but also in male authors' fiction. Appropriated in the literary works of the period to provide the internal historical and cultural coherence and the modern societal gender representation needed for national legitimation, women protagonists mark the inscription of the "feminine" as essential to nineteenth- and twentieth-century accounts of the Romanian nation. Far from being arbitrary constructions in the writings of such prominent novelists as Ion Agârbiceanu, Mihail Sadoveanu, Ioan Slavici, and Hortensia Papadat-Bengescu,[6] feminine protagonists are placed at the center of the narratives inviting an endless parade of new interpretations made possible by working from allegory and deconstruction.

While living within the boundaries of a man-made world, from the Transylvanian village of *Fefeleaga* to the Moldavian region traversed by shepherds in *The Hatchet*, through the small town community of *Mara* and well-traveled country roads converging at Ancuţa's Inn to the fashionable capital of Bucharest in 1920s Romania pictured in *The Disheveled Maidens*, the women protagonists I discuss are incorporated in fictional works as a way of combating (or socializing) the male-centered master discourse of the Romanian literary canon. Their experiences and literary representations start from enclosed spaces permitting small-group and face-to-face relations and lead to the modern city – a world without walls – in whose physical environment femininity turns out to be a referential structure, that is, a cultural sign of a modern nation. As they navigate through the traditional system of sociocultural and historical representation, these heroines stake a claim to that world by carving out their own paths until they cover every surface, change the structures they inhabit and ultimately take over more territory. Refusing the limitations imposed on them by patriarchal history and carried out in the name of irreducible gender differences, these female characters inhabit a space that dissolves into male structures and intertwines domestic and public comfort, making men at home in a world where women and men weave together the textures of language and fold themselves into a landscape that gives birth to a rich culture.

The works I have selected pry open the texture of historical and cultural evaluation and create a space for sociopolitical interpretations while engaging in a serious effort to (1) throw out the connotations obligatorily assigned to women (phallic shrew, object of desire, silent victim) in the Romanian patriarchal culture; (2) rearrange and replace the directionality of traditional criticism with a new and urgent emphasis on women as speaking and acting subjects for both men and women; and (3) illustrate the constellation of women protagonists in Romanian literature as part of a strategy of radical writing and reading empowering not only the emancipatory presence and unavoidable prominence of women within a modern culture, but also the attempt to consider feminine subjects as allegorical grounds for figurability when narrating the nation.

While it is obvious that female characters in Romanian fiction have their own particularity, it is nonetheless just as obvious that what defines them as women links them to other feminine characters that echo in a most specific way the universal traits and destiny of modern women and their struggle for sociocultural recognition. *Articulating Gender* is thus another step in this direction of examining the feminine voices that speak in important ways to the cultural complexities of a modern nation (defined not in the least in national and linguistic terms) and of valorizing their significance in the field of gender studies.

### *Notes*

1. See Ileana Orlich, *Silent Bodies: (Re)Discovering the Women of Romanian Short Fiction Translation and Critical Commentary* (Bucureşti: Editura Institutului Cultural Român, 2004).

2. Julia Kristeva, "Le temps des femmes," 33/34: *Cahiers de recherche de sciences des textes et documents*, no. 5 (Winter 1979); trans. Alice Jardine and Harry Blake, "Women's Time," *Signs* 7:I (Autumn 1981): 15.

3. *Ibid.*, 13-15.

4. Walter Benjamin, "The Work of Art in the Age of Mechanical Reproduction" in *Illuminations*, ed. Hannah Arendt; trans. Harry Zonh (New York: Schoken Books, 1968).

5. Terry Eagleton, "The Marxist Rabbi: Walter Benjamin," in *The Ideology of the Aesthetic* (Oxford: Blackwell, 1990): 316-40.

6. See Notes on Authors.

# Narrative Iconography and Metaphoricity
## in Agârbiceanu's *Fefeleaga*

In *Fefeleaga* (1908), Ion Agârbiceanu depicts the gloomy side of material and spiritual reality. Reflecting the economy's need for female labor in turn-of-the-century Romania, the impoverished Maria, the story's protagonist, becomes the head of the household and the bread-winner for her family after her husband Dinu's death. Every day of the week, including Sundays, she toils to get enough food for her five sickly children. In a weary succession of years, between deaths in her family – from her husband's to her last remaining daughter's – she drags her blind horse Bator to the bottom of the village's boulder-strewn hill where she fills up bags of gravel and carries them back into the village on Bator's back.

Throughout the story, the heroine's unselfishness and sacrificial spirit, which are contrasted with her late husband's evil character and with the incessant gossip of her mean-spirited neighbors, highlight Agârbiceanu's moralistic prose: the constant juxtaposition of the positive and negative values and the embedded sensitivity to human suffering metonymically reinforce the story's message. Like most of Agârbiceanu's short stories, *Fefeleaga* has a somber tonality in which the careful reader might correctly suspect a cleric's familiarity with homiletic forms addressed to village worshippers.[1]

The images of Fefeleaga, and the events surrounding her life, function as a referential structure used to formulate concepts about Christian life and beliefs. The heroine's downtrodden and dejected status, which wins her the unflattering nickname "Fefeleaga," an ono-matopoetic word suggesting the slow movement of the woman and her horse trudging toward the village with the gravel-loaded pouches, preserves the dictates of social verisimilitude while reaching icono-graphical proportions.

The mechanism required for the woman's image to take form and move within and through the words involves a putting into dis-course of the feminine that mediates the movement needed for the nar-rative to project itself into aesthetic representation. Rising and stooping,

Fefeleaga moves behind a screen of broken images that encode the dual representation of the text: the traditional image of the peasant-woman as a working mother/wife toiling from dawn to dusk to feed her family and the composition of her portrait that places Fefeleaga outside any social context and at a significant distance from the village space. Given the story's recognizable context of village life, Fefeleaga is nonetheless far from being a mere aesthetic representation aiming to express transcendental values. As an intersection of woman and iconographic metaphor, Fefeleaga's representation in the aesthetic realm is necessarily completed within the larger frame of her family life, her relationship with the village community and her closeness to her horse, Bator. In this dual stance, she expands the ancient connection between the woman and the land (Mother Earth) and the representation of motherhood echoed in Romanian religious icons, into the higher reaches of the iconographical system: Fefeleaga's fragmented corporeal representation – "tall, bony, with pock-marked cheeks deeply tanned by sun and wind, taking long strides in hardtop-boots, tramping noisily on the road, leading, or rather dragging, her white horse by the bridle"[2] – suggests a particular form of gynesis, taken to its extremes through the asceticism of a woman, whose exhausted representative mode "had to fold her back into the whisper of its own discourse."[3] Thus Fefeleaga's female body, which initiates a discourse of the feminine, makes possible the displacement of the structure of representation from a living person to the religious valorization of woman, strengthened through the technical evacuation of woman's body and "constituted," as Roland Barthes might say,[4] into something that approximates the Renaissance iconographic mode.[5]

One cannot understand the meaning of Fefeleaga's companion, the horse Bator, as a symbol of Romanian culture without referring to the iconography of Eastern Europe, in which the account of exploitation of horses ultimately serves as a form of estrangement or subjugation, an intensified metaphor of the human condition. A horse actually narrates Tolstoy's short story *Yardstick,* just as a horse narrates much of Solzhenitsyn's fifth film sequence in *August 1914,* in whose final shot the horse states:

But we horses are being caught. We are chased, and caught...
but we, the horses, shy away...but they again catch and rope...

> They are German soldiers, it's their orders, you wouldn't envy
> them – chasing horses, thousands of captured horses are lost.[6]

The next shot in Solzhenitsyn's text makes explicit the analogy
between horses and people, for it begins, "And not only horses." The
German soldiers round up and put into pens both horses and Russian
soldiers by the thousands.

A similar instance occurs in Agârbiceanu's story, when Fefeleaga
and Bator are analogously depicted:

> Both woman and horse had grown old. The woman's hair was
> grayish like the wool of the sheep. Deep lines wrinkled her pock-
> marked face. Her chin was growing angular: it had begun to point
> towards her mouth which had fallen inwards. The horse was still
> scraggier. The two earth-colored patches under the bags had
> grown larger; the hair on his ribs and back was even thinner. His
> lower lip hung downward as if stretched by an invisible load.
> (286)

This shadowy image of the woman and her horse silently coming
and going is clearly symbolic and has the effect of a *pars pro toto*: the
horse's shuffling bony shanks, covered with sores beneath the bags he
carries, convey the emotionally charged, timeless metaphor of physical
exhaustion, which echoes Fefeleaga's own deterioration and profound
alienation. Her estrangement suggests the unbelievable cruelty with
which the village community treats her and the sense of human cruelty
to other humans, which forces Fefeleaga to find in the horse her only
friend and companion. Left alone to care for five children after her husband's death, Fefeleaga draws strength and encouragement only from
Bator:

> As long as the dead man was still in the house, whenever
> Fefeleaga went into the yard it seemed to her that Bator, chewing
> away, was nodding his head and saying: "Yes, yes, yes. We'll do
> what we can." (284)

Accompanying this visual image, Fefeleaga's female strength
represents the moral cornerstone of the Romanian national type,
evincing an uncorrupted elemental force that reflects a Christian
archetype. Everything has gone wrong in Fefeleaga's life, from her

unhappy marriage to a physically and emotionally abusive husband to the deaths of all her children, probably because of tuberculosis. But even though she is burdened by external circumstances – poverty, loneliness, and the hardship of everyday life in a rural coal-mining community – her personality centers on Goodness and Charity. As a result of her five children's almost ritualistic deaths – they all die before they reach the age of fifteen – neighbors see Fefeleaga as a heathen:

> The old women of the village were whispering among themselves about her. They had heard this and that; maybe a few spells should be tried, for it smacked of the Unclean that her children kept dying, and all at the same age. (286)

Yet Fefeleaga is blessed with Christian virtues. She is unself-consciously righteous and pious, and a hard worker; work is her source of joy and spiritual balance. Indifferent to earthy possessions, she feels that her below-the-poverty-line income of three *zloty* a week "is enough to live on."[7] Respectful to all God's creatures, as illustrated by her caring attachment to her constant companion, the horse Bator, she bears no bitterness or anger toward anyone, but patiently endures whatever misery befalls her. She accepts God's plan with considerable strength, allowing even for injustices with humility and equanimity:

> But with the dead still in the house she would often go into the yard and speak to the horse: "How are you getting on, poor old Bator?" And the bony horse would shake his big head, as if saying: "Why fuss? That's the way of the world."
> And the horse was right! Such was the way of the world. Fefeleaga felt it sorely at the death of each child, with her house growing steadily emptier. (285)

Brought into strong relief throughout the story, Fefeleaga's character is Agârbiceanu's attempt to restore the lost outlines of an iconographic image, the concept of a viable ideal, one that is accessible and humane. Although suffering, Fefeleaga is nonetheless the story's restorative force, the bearer of the theme of its moral reformation. At this point, it is important to consider the ritual of sacrifice in European, and especially Romanian, ceremony as a fundamental act of religion, a gift or foundational event of the whole human civilization. In this sense, Agârbiceanu's text brings essential testimony to contemporary anthropology, which accepts sacrifice as a religious act modifying the moral condition of performers by consecrating them as victims – a formula largely embraced by the Romanian Orthodox Church.

But the core of Romania is above all problematic and ominously complex according to Agârbiceanu's perspective; its ideal incarnation, its mythopoetic *figura* Fefeleaga, is challenged symbolically by her late husband, Dinu, who had always beaten and cursed her, and by those who despise her. Blinded by their own vices to Maria's worth, the villagers, "scoffers as they are," (282) call her "Fefeleaga," a nickname which resonates with nothing human but which substantiates that the protagonist is excluded from language as a fundamental social bond. But in spite of these hardships Fefeleaga, who "had never wondered how much gold people made out of the gravel brought on Bator's back," (282) attains inner freedom and an exalted peace. Her daily work to support her children is done, and her ultimate comfort achieved in having Păunița, her last surviving child, buried in a painted coffin, with her head crowned with a bridal wreath and her virginal body wrapped in a diaphanous white sheet. As a latter-day Eastern European counterpart of a Pearl of great purity destined to heavenly glory, Păunița evokes the promise of a virgin's symbolic union with Christ in the celestial sphere, an image that speaks of the deep Christian faith associated with the Romanian national character. Having accepted her children's death as a manifestation of God's will, Fefeleaga provides an example of sainthood. Thus, in the final analysis, the story is a model for modern hagiography: Fefeleaga's virtues could and should be transplanted and thus preserved in Romania's rural community.

As the only preserver of the spiritual traditions among the village world, Fefeleaga leads an unnecessarily tragic life that stands not only as an ideal but also as a warning that her kind suffers in this world. Her tall, bony frame and her martyrdom double as symbols for a distorted community and announce the theme of disfiguration in the heart of Romanian culture suggested throughout the story, from the dysfunctional family to the gravel Fefeleaga hauls on Bator's worn-out back, which speak to the sterility of a land laid to waste. Distortion envelops all levels of the story, and a growing rumble of imagery announces a curse of disfiguration on this community. From the hill of barren boulders that stand as metaphors of abandonment to Fefeleaga's daily descent into a village that suggests a hellish pit, the landscape speaks of disfiguration.

In spite of these desolate images, however, Fefeleaga's grotesque appearance, battered by hardships and physical pain, has warmth and humanity. Her white horse is touched by her benign presence, spiritual health, and goodness, which seem powered by an organic earthly force. Plain and simple in her religiosity and ethic, she draws her strength from her selfless labor and her tragic plight: her luckless family life with Dinu, her children born and buried before they had a chance to mature, and the selling of Bator, her only friend and companion, to pay for her daughter's funeral. Indeed, with the loss of Bator the mood of the story turns apocalyptic. Destructive forces are overtaking traditional village life, tearing up the community. Fefeleaga's tragedy, in the end, is inseparable from the general social tragedy in Romanian rural life and from an elemental sense of alienation triggered by the loss of Christian values.

What dominates the consciousness in a reading of *Fefeleaga* is not only the title character's tragedy – an obvious symbol of a much larger significance – but rather the elemental and spectral quality of the living, for whom the dead are always awake, and the senseless and moral anarchy reaching deeply into the community. The story's tragic portrayal of Fefeleaga's life goes beyond her character. Woven into her destiny is the record of a community driven by crude impulses of greed and evil, a community that has accepted the ritual of Christianity but has remained alien to its ethic of love and self-sacrifice. On Sundays, for instance,

> the bitterness would gather in Fefeleaga's heart. It was then that she would collect her money for her week's work, and Bator's. The well-to-do, knowing she was alone in the world, did not pay regularly and did not even pay her in full; all of them owed Fefeleaga large arrears. They were sure she would come to work the following week, for she had to make use of Bator. They also reckoned that from one week to the other, Fefeleaga, being a woman, might forget. She did not forget but when she saw people were trying to deprive her of her modest due, she chose to say nothing. She never asked again (285).

The tragedy of botched life in *Fefeleaga* is all the more over-whelming because of the disparity between the real and the ideal that it exposes, not only in society at large, but also in man himself. In this connection, alongside the wealthy villagers who cheat Fefeleaga out of the money they owe her and who on Sundays "stay in the public houses, drinking beer instead of going to church" (285), is the figure of Dinu, Fefeleaga's husband, who occupies a central place in Agâr-biceanu's tableau of village life. The dark counterpart of Fefeleaga on the mythic as well as the real plane of the story, Dinu personifies the evil forces at the core of Romanian village life. His "wet and muddy" appearance, his work at the mine, and his drunken rages and cruelty – he threatens to kill his children because they are ill and coughing and because he cannot bear to see them so skinny – carry the motif of *demonism* in the story.

Like so many others around him, Dinu stands at the fringe of moral evolution, a troubled and uncertain realm where, as Fyodor Dostoevsky repeatedly demonstrates,[8] violence and sensuality consti-tute an entangling disease.

In such a world, Fefeleaga is the closest approximation to an ex-emplar of Christian redemption achieved through suffering. Ingrained in her endurance is the inexorable lesson of centuries: suffering must be borne because there is no way out. Thus her stoical passivity is not negotiated as a practical ethical-ideological stance, but is counterposed to the village world as a symbol of transcendent spirituality. Enshrined within her suffering, Fefeleaga emerges as a silent icon whose "smile seems strange on those pock-marked cheeks, which might have been likened to two gray small gray lumps pitted by the falling of many large raindrops" (285). Her stigmata, like those of her burdened beast, point to the possibility and direction of spiritual redemption.

The simplicity of the story's images, taken from everyday life, makes us wonder whether we should interpret them symbolically; but again, it is their simplicity that makes them successful symbols – clearly comprehensible signs of complex theological ideas or dogmas unexplained through logic. Invested with symbolic meaning, the story's apparently simplistic narrative elements become iconographic details emphasizing the role of Christian virtues in everyday life.

By attributing to Fefeleaga the Ten Christian Virtues depicted on the walls of many Transylvanian churches, the story attests to, and further enhances, the familiarity of the villagers with their Christian significance. By metaphorically removing the Ten Virtues from their icon settings or mural representations into the specific social and cultural context of late nineteenth-century rural Romania and by using Fefeleaga and her life as the story's conduit, Agârbiceanu relies on the underlying role of iconography to fuel his narrative, which in turn highlights various aspects of Romanian culture in a specific context and period.

Alongside Fefeleaga's association with Christian virtues is her representation as a suffering mother figure. Her particular bond with Mary the Mother of God, which is implied in her baptismal name, Maria, suggests that Fefeleaga is a holy woman blessed with many children, whose deaths are clearly intended to strengthen her iconographic stance. This view is certainly in line with traditional Eastern European Orthodoxy, in which children were the links between the divine, the saintly, and the laity. In Orthodox icons featuring children saints often appear with their hands raised in prayer or resting on the shoulders of the young they protect, substantiating the perception that children can be inherently blessed and that they may act as transmitters of faith in the family and the community, an avenue that offers access to the divine. After their deaths, children can be easily associated with the images of the saints and thus promote a sense of guardianship, where the holy figures intercede with God on their behalf or stand with them in solidarity and protection.[9]

A view that evokes the belief in a child's efficacy and predominance in religious practices was clearly comforting in the female-dominated world of church-worshippers at a time when child mortality rates were high.

In this context, Fefeleaga's role as the children's protector and nurturer is also important. Unlike Dinu, who beats and curses them because they are skinny and sickly, Fefeleaga brings love and comfort to her children:

> Whenever he [Dinu] came from the mine, wet and muddy, he started coughing and abusing the children because he couldn't endure seeing them so skinny. The woman took their part, comforted them, kissed their roughened white, little cheeks, which were always peeling.

"Let them alone," she would say, "what can you be expecting of them now? When they start working they'll get stronger." (283)

After selling Bator, Fefeleaga realizes that her feelings for the horse are ultimately a reflection of her love for her children:

She felt that her friendship for the horse, a friendship akin to the friendship for a human being, was due only to the help he had given her in looking after the children. And even now, the last bit of help came from Bator. Without him Păunița would have had no painted coffin, no bridal wreath, no white winding sheets. (288)

A secondary figure on the domestic front who merely witnesses a woman's rapport with her children and scorns her piety, Dinu highlights the ambivalent role of men in childrearing and the women's position of power in their childbearing and nurturing roles in Romanian communities. While the themes of men's minimal involvement in domestic life and women's dominant role in children's upbringing both as social beings and as individuals more embedded in the concrete are common in almost any cultural context, in *Fefeleaga* the heroine's devotion to her children is maximized as the most satisfying experience in her life.[10] As Fefeleaga comes to realize after the death of her last child, her love for her children had shaped her life:

Now she felt for the first time that she had nothing left to slave for. Not until the last of her children had died had she realized why she had kept it up. Now with Păunița lying there with the wax candle flickering at her bedside, Fefeleaga realized that it was for the sake of her children that she had endured it all. She alone knew what she had endured. But it had not gone against the grain; she had worked gladly! For them; first for five of them, then for four, then for three, for two, and in the end for one. The void in her soul had gaped wider whenever one of them had died, but her will to work did not subside. Two small tears the size of pinheads wet her dry eyes. (287)

Effectively constructed in the story, Fefeleaga's daughter Păunița suggests a further correspondence between Fefeleaga and Mary the Mother of God – the implication that the scorned woman's womb can be the bearer of a heavenly pearl. Presented in an intermediary state, neither a little girl nor quite a woman, Păunița is positioned between a physical and a conceptual reality that registers a state of transition between the two worlds, the earthly and the divine. Symbolic of both Păunița's body (human nature) and forthcoming royal dignity (divine nature), the white sheet and the bridal wreath that she wears in death place emphasis not only on the basic belief of a virgin's union with Christ as a celestial princess, but also symbolize Păunița's imminent reincarnation. The story's understood message, of course, is that all these heavenly privileges are guaranteed to a child raised in the faith. In the same vein, Fefeleaga's selling of her trusty Bator to buy for Păunița the beautiful burial wreath and cloth is an indication that she performs all the necessary acts of her faith to ensure God's continued benefi-cence on her departed child and on herself.

Fefeleaga articulates the idea of spiritual growth and stands for any maternal figure in the community. Her suffering, which is based on an essentially sacrificial relationship of separation and articulation of differences, stresses Fefeleaga's role and place in the story: left out of the sociocultural structure of the village community, she reveals the sacrificial spirit which is immediately recognizable and with which worshippers can identify, because it suggests the need for universal devotion to God and implies that faith and obedience bring rewards.

Both in their textual and their visual forms, all the images in the story express in simple terms the most basic aspects of the Christian Orthodox faith. The story's homiletic form suggests that Romanian village people were familiar with them and would recognize them in their discursive form as well, not simply because the narrative images echo the church icons, but because both illustrate the Romanian village and small town space at a particular time.

It is on this level of narrative iconography that the disparity of the real and the spiritual is bridged, suffering is redeemed, and the possi-bility of moral progress in society restored through faith, which is an affirmative answer to behavioral and ideological conformity upheld in the Christian community.

In *Fefeleaga* the act of narrative construction makes concrete (in language) the intention of the discourse, and this constructive activity is a function of what Paul Ricoeur calls metaphoricity.[11] Ricoeur's claims that we must move beyond a theory of metaphor as method of word substitution toward an interaction theory that stresses the "discursive" conception of metaphor, focuses attention on the metaphor as the unit of discourse. Unlike signs, which merely point to other signs, discourse – and by implication the metaphor – points to an extra-linguistic reality, which is its referent. Thus metaphor, an operation in which one thing stands for another, makes possible in Agârbiceanu's story a transference that establishes a tension and constitutes the modality of reference. More specifically, in *Fefeleaga,* metaphor does not merely bring about a simple transfer of words; it conducts a "transaction between contexts": Fefeleaga and the Ten Virtues; Fefeleaga and the religious icon; Dinu and the devil; and Păunița and the celestial glory reserved for holy innocents.

Through metaphoricity the story acquires a visual unity, one in which the single visual images of Fefeleaga and Păunița can be isolated, suggesting that worshippers could approach them individually for moral guidance and for prayer. They appear to function as devotional images akin to icons rather than as narrative elements, potential intermediaries through whom worshippers could communicate with the saints.

Beyond its metaphorical devices, the story's account of the inscriptions of social life in the village space reveals that they also have a substantial materiality conceived as a significant moment in the unfolding narrative of the nation seen as community. The need to bring the community's exclusive oppositions, Fefeleaga and the shallow villagers or Fefeleaga and Dinu, into unity calls for the reinforcement of models of goodness, purity, and unoppressive social and domestic relations as the normative ideal of Christian values. In radically opposing the social relations of an alienated community through the Christian values that she embodies, Fefeleaga detemporalizes the social milieu into a static spatiotemporality. With the elimination of these referential relations, the feminine protagonist's life and suffering acquire the dimension of a Christian parable that centers on Fefeleaga's figure to produce meaning through the scriptural spiraling of the literal and figurative that the text simultaneously carries.

## *Notes*

1. According to George Călinescu, Agârbiceanu's fiction discusses moral problems and usually follows the format of a homily. See *History of Romanian Literature* (Nagar Publisher, Bucharest 1994), 544-49.

2. Ion Agârbiceanu, *Fefeleaga,* in *Russian and Eastern European Literature*, eds. James Miller Jr., Robert O'Neal, Helen M. McDonnell (Glenview: Scott, Foreman, and Co. 1970), 281. All subsequent quotations are from this English translation of the story.

3. Gérard Genette, "Frontiers of Narrative," in *Figures of Literary Discourse*, trans. Alan Sheridan (New York: Columbia University Press, 1982), 143.

4. Roland Barthes, "Drame, poème, roman," in *Sollers écrivain* (Paris: Edition du Seuil, 1979), 11-45.

5. As stated in the essay, Fefeleaga's femininity, which is substantiated by the life context of the story, is not within the range of what Angelika Rauch discusses as a "usurpation of women for the mechanism of representation in the history of the aesthetic." "The *Trauerspiel* of the Prostituted Body, or Woman as Allegory of Modernity," *Cultural Critique* 10 (1988): 77-88.

6. In this polyphonic novel, which deals with the disastrous campaign against Germany of the Russian Second Army in the first days of World War I, the textual discourse is disrupted by the introduction into the writing of the "screen" passages of pseudo-film script, the historical documents and military communiqués, and of the extracts from contemporary newspapers that punctuate the fictional text with another kind of "factual" discourse.

7. A nickel coin equivalent to about 0.4 of a U.S. dollar.

8. Especially in *Crime and Punishment*, Dostoevsky's characters (Mikolka in Raskolnikov's dream about the beating of the mare) exhibit this sort of crude "ethic," which essentially claims that what one owns releases him from all obligations because it is one's property. And that includes, alongside one's material goods, the wife and children as well. For a detailed discussion of this problem, see "Philosophical Pro and Contra in Part One of *Crime and Punishment*," in *Twentieth Century Interpretations of "Crime and Punishment*," ed. Robert Louis Jackson (Englewood Cliffs, NJ: Prentice-Hall, Inc., 1974), 34-5.

9. For an expanded treatment of children in traditional Orthodox iconography, see Cecily Hennessy, "Iconic Images of Children in the Church of St. Demetrios, Thessaloniki," *Icon and Word: The Power of Images in Byzantium*, eds. Antony Eastmond and Liz James (Burlington: Ashgate Publishing Company, 2003), 157-73.

10. For an excellent discussion of the alignment of women and child bearing/child rearing with culture, see Sherry B. Ortner, "Is Female to Male as Nature is to Culture," *Woman, Culture and Society*, eds. Michelle Zimbalist Rosaldo and Louise Lamphere (Stanford, CA: Stanford UP, 1974), 79 and 81.

11. Paul Ricoeur, *Oneself as Another,* trans. Kathleen Blamey (Chicago: The University of Chicago Press, 1992).

# (De)Gendering the *Miorița* Ballad:
# Mihail Sadoveanu's *The Hatchet*

In *The Hatchet*[1] (1930), more than in any other of his great works, Sadoveanu captures the genius of folk culture, whose elemental forces determine the novel's system of images and artistic view of the world. Sadoveanu himself once described how he was inspired to write the story: while traveling in the country on a very hot day, he stopped at an inn to rest and to eat. At a nearby table he heard two policemen talking about a shepherd who had been killed and speculating as to who the murderer might be. The incident, which made Sadoveanu recall the *Miorița* plot, cast a retrospective light on the old folk ballad, which was to find its greatest literary expression in *The Hatchet*.

Viewed against the background of folk tradition, Sadoveanu's images in *The Hatchet* are completely at home within the centuries-old *Miorița* (The Little Ewe Lamb) ballad that is reconstructed in the novel's plot. Told and retold in countless versions, usually of about 123 short lines, *Miorița* is a nostalgic, lyrical tragic story of a shepherd's murder at the hands of two other shepherds who envy his wealth and kill him so that they can take ownership of his sheep. Even though he is forewarned by his beloved ewe lamb that he will be killed, the young shepherd accepts his destiny unquestioningly and begs the faithful ewe lamb to tell the other two shepherds to have him buried in the meadows near his sheep, so that he may be close to his beloved woods, the birds and the stars. He then asks the ewe lamb to urge everyone not to speak of his death but rather to tell everyone – especially his teary-eyed mother who will be looking for him – that he married a prince's daughter at heaven's gate.

With its mythic structure, submissive rhetoric and minimal narrative, *Miorița* is Romania's most enduring cultural text. In *Destinul culturii romînești*,[2] Mircea Eliade states that Romania has only two legends of its own, *Miorița* and *Master Builder Manole*, each preserved in "lyrical and ballad masterpieces. Of the two, however, it is probably *Miorița* that belongs most specifically to Romania, the *Master Builder Manole* legend having variants throughout the Balkan region in Macedonia, Bulgaria, and Greece. It is possible, however, that the *Miorița* legend has its origins in the Thracian myth of Orpheus" (25). In "*The Miorița*: An Introduction in the Form of a Memoir," Ernest H. Latham describes the *Miorița* "as the great defining ballad of the Romanian personality and culture. Thus it ranks in Romanian self-consciousness with the *Iliad* and the *Odyssey* for the Greeks, *Beowulf* for the Anglo-Saxons, the *Lay of the Host of Igor* for the Russians, the *Ballad of Kosovo* for the Serbs, *El Cid* for the Spanish, or the *Nibelungenlied* for the Germans."[3]

In a country long troubled by external conquerors and internal conflicts, the *Miorița* ballad may well be understood to convey the Romanian poetic imagination. Having to take refuge from the threats presented to the country's borders by escaping to its mountains and forests, Romanians are close to a nature they consider a sanctuary. According to Lucian Blaga, one of Romania's greatest poets and philosophers, the Romanian spirit is rooted in a mystical existence of reunion with nature and its contemplation, a condition which entails disregarding or ignoring history's temporal dimensions, but remaining conscious of one's own spiritual eternity.[4] Deriving his formulations from the *Miorița* ballad, Blaga defines the concept of the Mioritic space as delineating the specific geography of the Romanian poetic imagination. As one recent historian of the Romanians, Vlad Georgescu, summarizes it, *Miorița* is "a philosophical attempt to explain the Romanian spirit through the Romanian landscape, which Lucian Blaga saw as the stylistic matrix of Romanian culture."[5]

Turning the ballad's rhythmical pattern into a crisp prose style, *The Hatchet* tells the story of Nechifor Lipan, a well-to-do shepherd from the village of Măgura, who is murdered by two other shepherds, Ilie Cuțui and Calistrat Bogza, while the three men are journeying together toward the pasture where Nechifor wishes to leave his sheep for the winter. In Sadoveanu's story, however, Nechifor Lipan is the victim of a wicked plot and unexpectedly struck by the murderer, Calistrat Bogza, with a hatchet, from the back, while the other shepherd, Ilie Cuțui, keeps watch. Nechifor's body is then left to rot in a mountain ravine, prey to wild beasts and sinister ravens.

Worried that her husband has not returned home as he usually does after selling his sheep or taking them to warmer grazing lands for the winter, Nechifor's wife, Vitoria, decides to leave their home village of

Măgura high in the mountains to look for him. Accompanied by her son, Gheorghiţă, she plans to trace Nechifor's steps as she is reasonably sure, in spite of the assurances of the village priest, that her husband is long dead, murdered by thieves she wishes brought to justice. *The Hatchet* is thus her story, from the moment when she embarks on the long journey at the beginning of spring to the moment when she cleverly identifies both her husband's murderer and his accomplice, far away from her home but near the very site of the heinous crime that she manages to piece together ingeniously more than a year later.

As an exquisite adaptation of the folk ballad's gentle rhythms, rhyme-rich language and slow dynamics, Sadoveanu's work is above all an invitation for further analysis of *The Hatchet*'s production and narration within the novel's framework of modern culture and aesthetics. Famously identified by Blaga as the "Mioritic space," the matrix that typifies for Romanians a lingering memory of paradise, is an area or outer space known as *plai*, or the low foothills. Mentioned in the opening line of the *Mioriţa*, "Near a low hill/At heaven's doorsill," a *plai* is a weave of low hills and valleys, organically charting the journey of the soul toward an unspecified destiny from which there is no escape. Whoever has wandered on Romanian soil has certainly noticed the interwoven structure of its spaces: the shepherd lodgings stowed away on some mountain tops, with the villages scattered all the way down the valleys, a hill-valley rhythm and order that accounts for the overall appearance of villages not as discrete, compact units but rather as parts of units distanced from one another either by empty spaces or by the green aisles of yards and gardens, placed between houses and circling around shepherd lodgings at the top. Delineating this geography of the Romanian poetic imagination, the first image of *The Hatchet* introduces this same hill-valley pattern that mirrors *Mioriţa*'s landscape: "the village – which with its single cottages within fences of roughly hewn poles, lay scattered on the slopes descending abruptly from the fir woods – and the Tarcău – a mere rivulet, a flash of light deep down among the rocks" (5).

But although both the ballad and the novel invoke the traditional Romanian landscape, *The Hatchet* effects a displacement of perspective that reveals some important aesthetic and cultural differences between the two works. Whereas *Mioriţa*'s imagery represents a mythical, suspended landscape used as backdrop for the sacrificial image of a shepherd identified with the passive and accepting Romanian national selfhood, *The Hatchet* shifts and reframes its scenery to follow the sequence of events – the unraveling of a murder plot, the brutal killing of a shepherd at the hands of companions who must be tried and punished, and the need of a community to assert its normative values.

Inviting the reader to engage in further interpretation and reconstruction, the unforgettable figure of Vitoria Lipan presides over the habitually male folkloric domain and re-inscribes it within a gender-circumscribed linguistic and symbolic space. As she sits alone on the threshold of her village home, spinning in the autumn light, "her hazel eyes, in which the chestnut glint of her hair seemed to be reflected, held a faraway look. The spindle spun diligently as of its own accord…. Engulfed as in the darkness of night, her keen, still youthful eyes continued to scan the unexplored horizon" (5).

Prevailing over the village dwelling-places, Vitoria's photograph-like portrait and her spindle have an immediately modernizing impact and spin a different sort of narrative. The storytelling, in which male agency is attenuated from the start in the house denuded of a male occupant, comes with a degendering, or rather a "regendering" of the traditionally male-gendered Romanian folk ballad; the silent exclusion of the masculine turns Sadoveanu's text into a project to catch the essence of Vitoria Lipan. Thus *The Hatchet*'s reconfiguration reinterprets a folk ballad in terms of Romanian womanhood by both exploring its potential and severely undermining the patriarchal assumptions of a woman's limitations and traditionally passive role in that culture.

On a certain narrative level Sadoveanu's attempt to capture Vitoria Lipan is articulated in terms of finding an adequate language. The opening of the novel hints at the language of marriage as an institution meant to regularize the lives of individual persons by requiring virtues, or behaviors, that helped maintain the stability, as well as the harmony, of conjugal relations. In *The Hatchet*, the story that Nechifor Lipan always tells – a quasi-parable of the origin of various nations populating the earth – confers from the start its "nation as narration" quality which Sadoveanu craftily weaves into the text:

> Having made the world, the Lord God put order among the nations and gave each a distinctive sign.
> He taught the gypsy to play the fiddle and to the German he gave the screw....
> The Turk then came forward: "A rich share of wit thou shall not have, but by the sword shalt thou prevail over others."
> To the Serb he gave a spade...
> Finally the mountain people came and knelt before the Imperial Seat. The Lord God looked at them in pity:
> "And you, wretched folk," He said, "why are you so late?"
> "We are late, most hallowed Lord, because we came at the pace of our sheep and donkeys. We walk slowly, climbing up the steep path and descending low into the ravines. And in this way do we trudge along day and night, holding our peace, with the sheep bells alone making a clamor on the silent air. The dwelling-places of our wives and children are in the narrow clefts of the rocks, and lightning, thunder and torrents play havoc with us. We should like wide expanses, fields of corn and smooth-flowing waters."

"You are the last to come," the Lord said regretfully, "and dear though you are to me, I cannot help you. You will hold what you have, for I can give you nothing besides, except a light heart to rejoice at what is yours. Everything shall seem good to you; and always your door shall be open to the fiddle and the man with strong drinks; and your women shall be beautiful and full of love." (4)

The immediate purpose of the tale, however, is to introduce the absent Nechifor as a raconteur who "would tell now and again this tale at christenings and weddings of which he never missed a single one in winter time" (4). More importantly, the tale aims to present Lipan as a *pater familias* who looks at the world in general as tightly fitted into prepackaged boxes, and at his household in particular as his domain of paternalistic appropriation where the subaltern position of his wife, Vitoria, secures his mastery through her unconditional love for him. Married for more than twenty years to her husband and mother of their two grown children, a son Gheorghiță and a daughter Minodora, Vitoria is a victim more than once of her husband's rough drinking and womanizing, two of his favorite pursuits that allow for brief but unforgettable glimpses at the dark side of their life together. Determined to preserve her marriage by affirming behaviors and values that Romanian domesticity has traditionally appropriated, Vitoria is dedicated to her family, bears Nechifor's beatings "without flinching," and counters with her own "devilish temper." Still, and especially whenever he "hung his head and showed great sorrow," she found that she was still in love with his "black mustache, those eyes with slanting eyebrows, [and] his squarely-built, broad-shouldered figure" (6). During Nechifor's prolonged absence, she reminisces on the highs and the lows of their life together:

It would be nine years on St. George's Day since she had jumped at him like a tiger-cat trying to get at his eyes and throat with her nails. He had pushed her gently aside with his arm and laughed. She had grown fiercer then, reproaching him with "that ugly slut" from somewhere at the mouth of the Tarcău.

"That's where you go and spend your money," she had flung at him with other bitter things, and again had tried to get her claws into him. He had struck her then, after which he had drawn her to

his breast and held her tight. She had become silent at that and as
still as if she had died, her forehead closely pressed under his arm,
and she had waited for his caresses like a wretch.

Seven years ago he had struck her on account of another
woman. One year it had been dark eyes, the next the blue eyes of a
German. She understood in a way that for a man like him it was
merely a pastime – just as he would drink a glass of wine or break
through the branch of a tree in passing. (53)

It seems that Vitoria's privileged moments occur when silence
encroaches, and so her power over her husband comes with her
manipulation of him through deliberate self-suppression as the cardinal
virtue. In their marriage, she relies little on language, and her discourse
with life is when words disappear and her personality and selfhood can
assert themselves:

Vitoria had her reckonings with Lipan. She had much to say to
him, and said it without moving her lips or her tongue. She said it
all deep down within herself – with all the old suspicion and
suffering. (52)

But while she acknowledges Nechifor's womanizing and drinking
to those who knew him, Vitoria also greatly admires her husband as a
courageous and fearless man. In the brief story that she tells Mr. David,
the shopkeeper, and his wife early on, at the beginning of her journey,
Vitoria eerily anticipates the manner in which Nechifor had been murdered (by being thrown into a ravine) and correctly anticipates that only
friends could ever harm him by attacking him behind his back:

"Indeed he was a wayward man in his cups," Vitoria admitted. "I
loved to see him so brave and bold. Nobody could oppose him.
One day, when we were returning from Piatra, when I was pregnant with Gheorghiță here, some people with their faces smeared
with soot held us up. They raised their cudgels against us and
demanded our money and the food we carried. They had come
upon us at night in a gully at a bend in the road. But Nechifor had
his hatchet with him. He took off his fur cap, threw back his head
and seized the hatchet. 'You cowards,' he shouted, 'I will smite
you in the Lord's name and kick you into the ravine.' The men
fled behind some bushes and disappeared. No, he wasn't afraid of

robbers, for he knew how to deal with them. Only if friends had struck him treacherously from behind could he have been brought down." (51)

Because her husband had always come back home to her in spite of his philandering – "She had been above them all [the other women]; she had possessed a power and a secret which Lipan had not been able to guess at. And he had come home to her as one comes to a refreshing spring" (53) – Vitoria consults with both the priest and the village sorceress when Nechifor fails to come home in the fall. But later during the winter, when she fights back her tears and obediently follows both pagan and Christian rituals in making offerings to the church saints, to the priest, and to the old sorceress and in "fasting for twelve Fridays in succession" (23), Vitoria begins to suspect that her husband must have perished.

In spite of the village men talking at the inn and spreading the word that Nechifor is "a deserter and had run away from his wife" (46) and taken aback by the village sorceress who advices "trying charms and working on waxen figures" (27), Vitoria reveals her secret fears to her son:

> "I keep turning things over in my mind, and I dream a dream which saps my health and makes and old woman of me. Something has happened to him and I shudder to think what." (26-7)

When we first see Vitoria, she is turning her spindle as a symbolic, reflexive act underlying a certain discoursivity. The structure of that reflection is her yielding of herself to the world of things and human relations as she builds a second world and a second life outside the domestic realm, a world in which she, the traditionally gendered subaltern, is assigned a new subject position. After fasting and walking aimlessly with a black kerchief drawn over her mouth and after considering herself as dead to the world as the man who was absent from her side, she realizes that "her love was the same as in her youth" (28) and that she must actively look for a resolution to the crisis brought about by her husband's disappearance.

As Vitoria prepares for the long journey to find her husband, or what is left of him "so that she might take him from the place of his destruction and lay him in holy ground, with all the customary rites"

(87), she first handles all the family business. In this new stance of a subaltern gender turned into the new head of the household, Vitoria holds a certain glamour. She settles the accounts with the shepherds and sells the sheepskins, lambskins, and the smoked and salted cheeses with such ability that she makes Mr. David, the shop owner from the neighboring town who buys her produce, exclaim to Mr. Iordan, the clerk brokering the transaction,

> "I'll tell you something, Mr. Iordan," he [Mr. David] whispered drawing close to the clerk's shoulder and shutting his right eye. "If I were not a Jew and married, and this woman had no husband, there'd be a wedding in a week. Father Danilă [the village priest] would marry us. I am taking the goods and am paying you the commission you asked for in your letter." (42)

After setting her house and the business in order, Vitoria sends her daughter to a convent for protection and then arms her young son, who is to accompany her on the journey, with a new hatchet, a symbol of Vitoria's own hatchet-sharp mind and will to find and punish those who might have harmed her husband. To her son's question, "But how long will we stop whenever we're going?" she answers, "Not anywhere for long. We will keep going until we find what we are after. We have no other plan. And don't forget to sharpen the hatchet. We will need a reliable weapon" (44).

Her journey through valleys and hills, her frequent stops at road-side inns, and her shrewd and daring behavior are told in the dynamic tone of a communicative context that draws the reader inside the action, a radical departure from the ballad's submissive tone and aesthetic transparency. Although shaped by patriarchal ideology that has assigned her in the past to domestic roles only, with the sexual division of labor and authority now reversed Vitoria becomes an agent of transition from the domestic/private to the civil/public spheres. Thus, if *The Hatchet* displaces the traditional domestic domain, it also dramatizes its shifting connection to women's social emancipation through Vitoria's movement outside of patriarchal control. When she stops at Mr. David's inn, Vitoria projects the image of a "mountain woman," ready to act like a man, in control and ready to defend herself if necessary:

> At Călugăreni, close to the Piatra Teiului, Mr. David had his abode behind a shop and an inn. His wife came to meet him, with flesh of milky whiteness and double chin, and spoke her joy in a lilting voice. Her eyes opened wide when the woman from the mountains took a sawn-off shot-gun, such as thieves are known to possess, from behind her saddle. (50)

At Mr. David's inn Vitoria hears more about her husband's boldness and fondness for wine and revelry. The innkeeper tells the story of a rock (Piatra Craiului) high up on a mountain peak, said to have been planted there by the devil with the intention of hauling it back into the Bistrița River to dam the water and drown the village before God stopped this evil plan. According to Mr. David, whenever Nechifor stopped at the inn, "he always wanted to climb to the top and mark it with his axe against the devil. He would shout that he wanted a pitcher of wine to take with him and the musicians as well" (51).

More is heard about Nechifor from Old Man Pricop at whose house Vitoria and her son find shelter on their continuing journey. After praising Nechifor as "a fine man," the old man adds,

> "Only one thing I didn't like about him: his going on his way at night. It would have been my pleasure to hobnob with him as I do with you. I don't do it with the other villagers but I like to welcome strangers, for they're only passing, and maybe they have troubles; and it's a good thing to hand them a sweet drink and a kind word. But that man said he would travel by night as he enjoyed riding in the moonlight and didn't fear the wicked of the world for he had pistols for them in his bag." (59)

The purpose of these stories is to portray the absent Nechifor as a strong and memorable character, matched in all his manly qualities by his wife's own courage and intelligence, an aspect which is really the novel's central interest. Thus Vitoria's story is *not* that of the singular development of a feminine subjectivity, a female Bildungsroman. Her journey, which marks the progress of the subaltern in a subject-position, is a discursive terrain necessary to highlight her potential as an individual of equal human value in her own way to her husband. To underestimate or dismiss Vitoria's actions and innermost thoughts as those of an illiterate peasant woman, and not to perceive her as equally valuable to her community as her able and shrewd husband once was, is to fail to understand the underlying message of Sadoveanu's novel and to distort the picture of the community it projects.

Deepened and rendered more complex through the storytelling, Vitoria's actions and thoughts mirror the Romanian rural landscape upon which the life of the community is acted out. Grasping the social and topographical texture of the countryside that the heroine traverses, Vitoria's presence mediates between the readers and the events establishing the credibility of the latter to the former. In this sense the christening and the wedding Vitoria encounters become a piece of testimony with a status equivalent to a public document or written history – an instrument of proof to authenticate the nation through the human geography of the village life and its ancient customs. As the next two quotations show, Vitoria's journey is also both an act of religious significance and a means to exhibit economic status, as she and her son engage meaningfully in the rituals of the villages through which they pass:

> At Borca they came upon a christening. People came out to meet them, took hold of the horses' halters and led them into a courtyard. With flushed faces, they took pleasure in treating the wayfarers to their goodly fare. Vitoria was forced to dismount and enter the house to see the young mother, under whose pillow she slipped a little bag of sugar lumps, while on the forehead of the new-born babe she placed a twenty lei banknote. She raised her glass to the godfathers, and kissed the hand of the priest. (60)

*   *   *

> At Cruci they came upon a wedding procession. The sledges carrying the wedding guests glided swiftly over the ice of the Bistrița. The bride and the bridesmaids had flowers in their hair, while the married women wore only short furred coats over their peasant skirts. The men fired their pistols at the fir trees to scare away winter before its proper time and, as soon as they caught sight of the strangers on the upper road, youths were specially appointed to invite the guests, and spurred on their horses to meet them, the ornaments on the horses' ears waving in the wind. They held out their flasks of liquor and raised their pistols: either they

would drink in honor of the lordly bridegroom and of the most worthy bride, or be killed on the spot.

The wedding procession wound its way along the high road, while Vitoria accepted the flask and wished the bride joy. Her face took on a pleasant look and her tongue wagged merrily.... (61)

Continuing her journey, Vitoria finds people who can bring further testimony of Nechifor's passing along the way, villagers who remember him vividly as "a man with a grey fur cap, riding a black horse with a star on its forehead." In Vatra-Dornei, the town of Nechifor's would-be destination to buy the sheep at the fair, Vitoria learns from a German clerk that a purchase of 300 sheep had indeed been made the previous autumn and that the buyer had been her husband. She also learns that on the spot Nechifor had sold 100 of the sheep to two husbandmen, asking for only a small profit for himself and joining the two men on their continuing journey. At one of her next stops, in the village of Sabasa, Vitoria hears that Nechifor and the two husbandmen – one "of a small build and swarthy, the other burlier and with a harelip" (69) – had really bonded and seemed to be enjoying each other's company. She then crosses the steep and lonely Stînişoara Mountain "through a winding path cut in the rock, with vultures hovering above a wilderness of ice and snow" (72), only to find out in the next village, Suha, that Nechifor is no longer seen in the company of the two husbandmen.

From Mr. Toma, the village innkeeper, and his wife Maria, Vitoria learns the two men's names and marvels when she hears about their sudden wealth from the innkeeper's wife – the great number of sheep they had purchased from a wealthy man who had sold them his entire flock before heading back to his own faraway home. To fuel Vitoria's dark suspicions at this point, Nechifor's dog Lupu is found at a village house. Next comes the terrifying moment when, led by the dog, Vitoria and Gheorghiţă come upon Nechifor's remains in a steep ravine. With the dog racing around the mountain steep side and then rushing upon Gheorghiţă and seizing him by his coat,

> The blood rushed to the woman's [Vitoria's] face and her eyes shone. The boy understood. Rounding the stone parapet, he let himself slide down the abrupt slope. The woman leaned over and looked into the precipice. Gheorghiţă was sliding smoothly as he

went. The dog could no longer be seen. His bark alone was heard from the ravine.

She caught sight of the boy skirting the foot of the slope. Then, suddenly, his fearful cry rose towards her. Sure of what was there, Vitoria gathered her skirts about her legs and let herself slide down as the boy had done. Her head in a whirl, she landed at the foot of the slope amidst the sharp, angry barking of the dog. Gheorghiță was sobbing, his right arm flung across his eyes. Scattered bones with their wet joints made white patches on the ground. The boots, pouch, thick leather-belt and grey fur cap were Nechifor's. And he was there too – at least what the wild beasts' fangs had left of him. The skeleton of the horse, picked clean of flesh, lay a little further away under the saddle and the rugs. The man's skull, she saw, had been broken by a hatchet. (93)

A charged place, haunted by the dead man's ghost, the site of Nechifor's remains appropriate the landscape as the soul of the murdered shepherd seems to be lodged into his belongings. While making identification possible, "the boots, pouch, thick leather-belt and grey fur cap" account for an extraordinary visualization that prompts Gheorghiță's sobs and Vitoria's hasty actions. Tearlessly, she performs "the first rites" by "take[ing] a rug from among the moist, moldy things that had been Nechifor Lipan's and lay[ing] it over his remains" (93). As part of the same initial ritual, she then fumbles among her things and, after finding matches and a waxen candle, she lights the candle and places it near the bones.

Before she can punish those whom she rightfully suspects of her husband's murder, however, Vitoria first has to plan Nechifor's funeral, a ritual that must occur to pacify the spirit of the dead man who "was waiting for the last blessing and the prayers which had not been said for him yet" (95). Consisting of lamenting the deceased, the funeral is a reflection of Romanian folk culture, a mixture of religious and pagan rituals, of mysticism and piety, intricately paired inside the Romanian Orthodox Church's rites involved in the burial of the dead.

Because Nechifor's bones must be examined for evidence of murder by the local authorities, Vitoria summons the priest and mourners to the ravine first. Here she pours brandy for them and they all take turns drinking from one glass, each time remembering before drinking to raise the glass to the memory of the dead. To feed those who come to see the dead and keep vigil over him, a man Vitoria hires brings "twenty loaves of bread, four pounds of olives, ten herrings and five pint jugs of brandy." And the innkeeper, Mr. Toma, according to custom, speaks words that soothe Vitoria's heart: "May God forgive all Nechifor Lipan's trespasses, done with or without his will; and may He kindly give him rest in the earth, from now on at least." In the end, as the priests puts on his stole, strokes his white beard and begins to read the prayers, Vitoria "removes a corner of the rug that the dead, too, might hear the prayers, and look skyward with the black orbs of his skull" (97).

One of the main purposes of the whole ritual, at the murder site and during the burial, is to set right the dead man's impious end and to glorify the deceased. When Nechifor is found, the degradation suffered by his body hurled into the void of the ravine and his roaming spirit "risen every night to his feet, clad in the rug" (95) must be transformed into regenerating value and overcome through ritual into a new birth. After the removal of Nechifor's bones from the ravine, they are sanctified through the funeral rites. That process, which includes strong elements of dramatic display, such as the washing of the bones, the crying of the hired mourners, and the priests' sprinkling of the bones with holy water, resembles an elaborate spectacle, with specific roles to be performed by all participants, from the widow to the mourners.

With the help of the women from the Sabasa, Vitoria makes sure that everything takes place according to custom:

> Seldom in Sabasa had there been such a service as that held for the dead man. The golden April sun beat down obliquely on the uncovered remains of Nechifor Lipan. The priests prayed to the Lord God to give peace to the soul of His servant, Nechifor, and then raised their strong voices to sing the requiem. Vitoria came up to Mistress Maria and asked her hurriedly to see that every rite was performed to the very end. In particular, she was not to forget to ask for the wine at the right moment, to sprinkle over the remains of the dead man. ...She begged Mistress Maria to do her this great favor, as she herself had to be at her husband's side at the moment of leave-taking. This would be her last chance to look upon him. After that she would see him only on the Great Judgment Day. (110)

Marking the final event in the ritual of the dead, the commemorative feast Vitoria gives immediately after the funeral service celebrates Nechifor's luminous memory and his cosmic transformation into an incandescent, positive force in the afterlife – something not that much different from the celestial glory the young slain shepherd in the *Mioriţa* ballad envisions for himself when he asks the little ewe lamb to present his death to his mother as a wedding to a heavenly princess. By contrast with the glorified deceased, the two murderers Calistrat Bogza and Ilie Cuţui, whom Vitoria insists on inviting with their wives to the feast following the burial, degrade the ceremonial through their mere physical presence. Their excessive drinking and Bogza's harelip convey their grotesque,[6] debased and alienating characters defined by a vulgar sense of egotistic possession lurking behind their recently accumulated wealth. Seated toward the lower end of the huge table, the two appear cut off from the other guests, as blunt and reprehensible as their flippant conversation. In their degrading isolation, Calistrat Bogza and Ilie Cuţui are coarse and deadly obstacles to the collective celebration and their presence is seen as the element of negation, breaking the continually renewed link with a cosmic regenerating force.

As food and drinks flow freely, this feast, which is an event legalized outside the official sphere and in which all guests take part as if there is no life outside it, becomes another spectacle in itself. Subject to its own laws, that is, the unbroken and living laws of the folk culture free of the official way of life or of any agency outside it, the festivity marks the suspension of all hierarchical rank, privileges, norms, and prohibitions and upholds the community as the voice of ultimate authority. In her role of widow, Vitoria is fully aware that this could well be the scene outside the established order where she may have to act as the judge and executioner of her late husband's murderer, especially since the local authorities represented by the assistant police chief Anastase Balmez seem to be inefficient in the investigation of the murder. She knows that the special form of free and familiar contact customary at such community gatherings will suspend the barriers of gender distinctions and hierarchical rank in favor of a utopian realm of freedom and equality where there are no delegated powers; and she is confident that this setting will also create a type of communication impossible in everyday life where officials, such as Mr. Balmez, "think it beneath their dignity to admit that a woman is right" (101).

But even Mr. Balmez finally has no choice but to consider Vitoria "a shrewd and secretive woman," especially after her insistence that Ilie Cuțui and Calistrat Bogza be invited to the funeral feast prompts him into thinking that the two men's presence could be "a discreet and wary investigation to discover and lay his hands on the criminals." More importantly, as Mr. Balmez reasons, "the two husbandmen could not refuse to come to the burial at Sabasa. That was what in law books is called confronting them with the corpse of the victim" (101). And although Vitoria, when told of Mr. Balmez's decision to invite the two suspects to the feast, did not know what "confronting them with the corpse actually signified, she accepted the decision of the authorities with a smile. For even though Mr. Balmez was a gentleman and one conceited at that, she [Vitoria] and Mistress Maria could get the better of him and twist him around their fingers, together with the doctor, Bogza, Cuțui, their wives and all" (102).

Of overwhelming importance in this setting is the community, whose cohesive unity of tradition and historical continuity confers upon Vitoria the authority she needs before she can make her accusatory move. As a widow and an equal sharer in Nechifor's legacy, "the mountain woman" has every right to unmask and punish his murderers. And she begins to do so by moving toward the low end of the table where the two are sitting during the feast. Once seated near Calistrat Bogza, Vitoria begins to examine his hatchet (which she instinctively recognizes as the murder weapon) and then begins to tell her tale of how Nechifor must have been murdered:

> "Well, it was like this, Mr. Calistrat. My husband was thinking of his affairs and of me, and was riding uphill towards the Talians' Cross, his horse going at an amble. Some might say that he was coming down the mountain. But I know better; he was going up. And he was not alone! He had the dog with him. And there were two men as well. One of them had spurred his horse to the top, to see whether anyone else was in sight. The second walked behind Nechifor, leading his horse by the halter. And it was not yet night. Only dusk. Some think that such deeds are done at night, but I know that this was done while there was still daylight, towards sunset. When the man on the hilltop signaled to show that no one was about and his companion need have no fear, the man who walked let go of the horse's reins and drew the hatchet from under

his left arm. Advancing stealthily across the path, he came right
behind Nechifor Lipan. He struck him just one blow – but a
mighty one, that would have cleft a tree trunk. Lipan threw up his
hands. He did not even have time to shout; he just fell forward, his
face in the horse's mane. Turning the hatchet, the man pushed the
horse with it into the ravine. It was then that the dog sprang at
him. He kicked it in the jaw. The horse had been frightened and,
when it was pushed, rolled down the slope. The dog went that
way, too." (113-4)

When she finishes giving her flawless account of the murder,
which she claims was whispered to her by her husband's own ghost in
the ravine while she kept watch over his corpse, everyone becomes
tense and Bogza, the murderer, feels cornered:

> All present sat as if petrified, rooted in suspense. All the people
> here had their suspicions. The reports and intrigues had done their
> work. So everybody understood, at least in part, the gist of the
> mountain woman's tale.
> And Calistrat Bogza was thinking much the same thoughts.…
> He would be a stupid fool to believe that she had been present.
> And a still greater fool to think that the dead man has spoken.
> Nowadays nobody believed such things, and yet this woman
> showed him everything as if it had happened, point by point and
> step by step.
> While these thoughts raced through his mind, Bogza drank
> down one glass of wine after another, for he felt the people's eyes
> on him. (114-5)

As the story's emotional content rises, the murderer's psychic
tension can be felt. And even though we as readers are not allowed to
enter the characters' minds, we intuitively feel the negative energy and
pent-up tension that inhabits the space of the feast. The staccato and ir-
regular prose style, the disjointed ensuing conversation between Bogza
and Vitoria, the references to Bogza's hatchet and the looping back into
the story to the one Nechifor always carried on him – all these communicate disruptions in the normal flow of the funeral feast and announce
the impending violence of the final reckoning. Once Vitoria, upon
examining Bogza's hatchet, exclaims to her son, faking surprise,
"Gheorghiță, I think there's blood on that hatchet and that this is the

man who struck your father!" (116), the murderer is overcome with sheer hatred for the woman who denounces him. As he tries to attack Gheorghiță, the young man strikes Bogza on the forehead with the hatchet leaving him enough time only to confess to the priest that he had indeed murdered Nechifor, "exactly as the dead man's wife has said" (117).

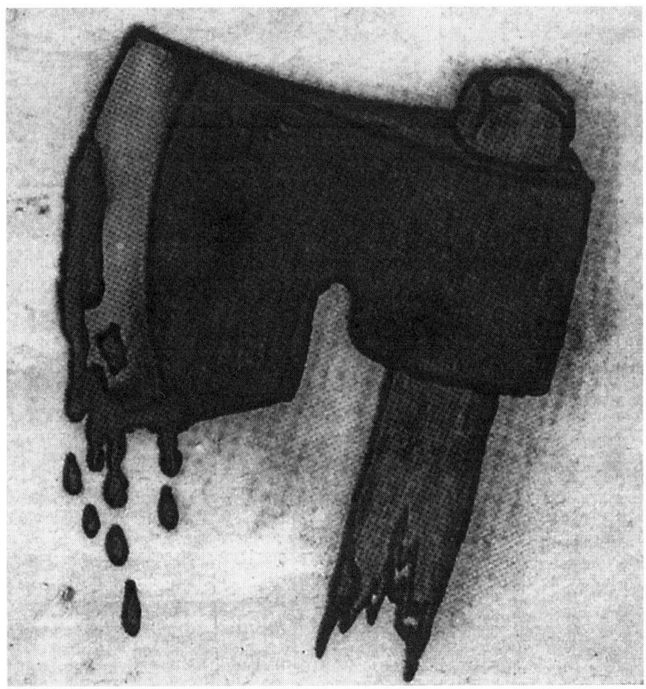

To settle Nechifor's murder, Vitoria places her reckoning with Calistrat Bogza in the hands of her son. Appealing to her biological link with her son, she uses his arm and ability in the service of their common cause as a means of redressing the injustice done to their family. In a clever reversal of traditional paternity that enables a father to appropriate a son as an extension of his being, Vitoria relies on her motherhood to overcome the physical limits of her body by appropriating her son's body as an extension of her own being. The conceit that mediates the mother-son bond through its physical intervention marks the absence of the father's body and renders the mother and the son indistinguishable as separate persons. Notably, the female body, which traditionally disenfranchises women and reduces them to a mere reproductive function, acquires through this conceit a new dimension in the system of social reproduction, whereby the woman mother is no longer just a physical body; rather Vitoria's role and function must be understood as the logical extension of the patriarchal position that underlies social traditions. Vitoria's action of summoning her son to avenge the injustice done to their shared blood, marks the radical erasure of her physical body as a commodity in and of itself, and establishes the mother as an empowered authority, with a new political status: as the uncontested head of the family, she formulates her demand for revenge, "There is blood on that hatchet," which is a clear allusion to the established social system that requires immediate action and swift punishment. What all that means is that by not punishing the murderer, Nechifor's family will symbolically lose all its economic interests and social standing in the community.

When Vitoria perceives the hatchet to be covered with Nechifor's blood and thus, following the implicit logic of the scene, to be tainted to the family blood, the subtext of the narrative indicates that the only possible reconciliation requires the shedding of the murderer's own blood. And so when Vitoria indirectly assumes the position of judge executioner, since she considers Bogza's death to be the only appropriate punishment for Nechifor's murder, she upholds the abstract legitimacy of the law – and in the process establishes her identity as a new political force within her family and society.

With the ending of the novel announcing Vitoria's humorous opposition to her daughter's marriage to the village church psalm singer's son with whom the girl is in love, *The Hatchet* ends not with a burial but with the anticipation of a wedding, a sign that equilibrium has been reestablished. This forthcoming celebration, in which Vitoria will again have the final decision-making power, is the finishing touch to a personal story functioning as a national allegory. Having been used on an immediate level as a backdrop for an idealized female subjectivity, *The Hatchet* gradually subordinates Vitoria's personal narrative to the national narrative by re-inscribing the *Miorița* ballad in the space of modern Romania. In this context, Vitoria Lipan increasingly becomes the instrument for fashioning a "modern" Romanian woman. Unlike the absent feminine character in *Miorița*, the shepherd's mother who presumably accepts her son's death unconditionally, Vitoria Lipan goes boldly in her search for the murderers of her husband. Her journey takes her far away from her village and her encounters with various people along the way sharpen her physical endurance and creative intelligence while highlighting her womanhood as part of the natural order of things.

In addition to the obvious differences in the development of the plot, far from being a mere re-telling of the *Miorița* ballad, *The Hatchet*'s fast-paced drama is a significant revision of traditional representations and resonates with the feminist model of relating femininity to authority. Having lost her husband, Vitoria can now partake of the kindness and friendship of the new people she encounters, and she seems to be as well-liked by strangers as he once was, exchanging her traditional femininity for a rewarding homosociality[7] once enjoyed only by males. This new capacity gives Vitoria's public actions the legitimacy that will then enable her to denounce her husband's murderers – not as a wronged woman, but as an individual voice assimilated within the community. Thus *The Hatchet*'s fictional world signals the story's departure from self-possessive feminism and simply celebrates Vitoria Lipan as someone who transcends patriarchal history and obtains complete self-emancipation to bring to justice two murderers responsible for the social disruption that the slaying of a friendly and generous man brings to the imagined space of the community seen as a nation.

In the traditional culture of Romania, a country divided for many centuries during its long and turbulent history, the community is never an abstract concept, but a concrete, social framework sustained by specific human relations between husband and wife, parent and child, older brother and younger brother, and, above all, one friend and another. Such a formulation defines an individual as a relational being and positions him or her in reciprocal obligations to others in the family, the clan, the society. If the *Miorița* gives its readers a clear sense of the folk ballad's evolution into an instrument for ideological struggles, a process in which the ballad was constantly rewritten in versions that serve specific political premises, *The Hatchet* regulates the behavior of individual persons by requiring virtues that helped maintain the stability, as well as the harmony, of social relations. Although asserting as central the cardinal virtue of marital fidelity and moral integrity, *The Hatchet* also brings into relief Vitoria's quest for and public denunciation of her husband's murderers in order to restore both social order and the rule of justice. Her actions, loyalty to the memory of her husband, and determination help maintain the continuity of a set of social relations that begins in the family and ends in the absolute authority of the community (which regards the family as its foundational unit) seen as a nation.

In final analysis Sadoveanu's recreation of the *Miorița* ballad in *The Hatchet* involves two narratives: Vitoria's personal narrative that openly celebrates her strength and wisdom by asserting that women are often stronger than men, and a national narrative designed to give Vitoria's story a sort of authenticity by placing her actions in a specific social context. As the story line develops, Vitoria's personal narrative is gradually subordinated to the national narrative, and the individual heroine increasingly becomes simply the instrument for fashioning a new woman, one capable of protecting and controlling her own life and family. In the process, *The Hatchet* offers a vibrant insight into Romanian culture that is collected, concentrated and artistically rendered to reconstruct our entire artistic and ideological perceptions, especially in regard to women, tradition, and nation building.

### Notes

1. Mihail Sadoveanu, *The Hatchet*, trans. Eugenia Farca, in *Classics of Romanian Literature*, Volume III, (Boulder and New York: East European Monographs/Columbia University Press, 1991). All quotations are from this edition.

2. *The Fate of Romanian Culture*, trans. Bogdan Ştefănescu (Bucureşti: Editura Athena, 1995).

3. Ernest H. Latham, *Miorița: An Icon of Romanian Culture* (Iaşi: The Center for Romanian Studies, 1999). Quotations from the *Miorița* ballad are from this bilingual edition.

4. Lucian Blaga, *Trilogia culturii* [The Trilogy of Culture] (Bucureşti: Editura pentru Literatură Universală, 1969), 119-31.

5. Vlad Georgescu, *The Romanians: A History*, ed. Matei Călinescu, trans. Alexandra Bley-Vroman (Columbus: Ohio State Press, 1991), 205.

6. I have in mind that trait of grotesque which W. Kayser in *Das Grotesk in Malerei and Dichtung* identifies with its hostile and inhuman possibilities.

7. I am using Eve Kosofsky Sedgwick's concept of homosociality to designate "the social bond between persons of the same sex; it is a neologism, obviously formed by analogy with 'homosexual,' and just as obviously meant to be distinguished from 'homosexual.' In fact, it is applied to such activities as 'male bonding,' which may be characterized by intense homophobia, fear and hatred of homosexuality." *Between Men: English Literature and Male Homosocial Desire* (New York: Columbia University Press, 1985), XIII.

# Ioan Slavici's *Mara*: A Woman's Life

Ioan Slavici's *Mara* was published serially in the first twenty-four issues of the literary journal *Vatra* (The Hearth) beginning in 1894. Published as a novel in 1906, *Mara* distinguishes itself as a masterpiece of "classical harmony in its narrative structure [that] offers the most comprehensive panoramic view of the rural community of Transylvania in the second half of the nineteenth century."[1]

The novel's narrative plot situates the impoverished widow Mara and her two children – a daughter Persida and a son Trică – at the heart of the changing landscape of Banat, a border region of western Transylvania that was at the time of the narrative under Austrian control.[2] A dynamic marginocentric node of Orthodox, Catholic, Reformed, and Lutheran Christianity connecting Central Europe with the Balkans, and a liminal zone where Romanians represent the largest ethnolinguistic group, Banat has traditionally evinced a hybrid Central Eastern European identity and a baroque approach to culture. Already in the eighteenth century, the area could boast "a developed system of mining, river transportation, sewage systems and canals, trade companies…and schools in Romanian, German, Hungarian, Serbian, Hebrew."[3] As Marcel Corniş-Pope notes, Banat's "ethnic and cultural pluralism stimulated competitive/cooperative modes of development beneficial to all groups…craftsmen and farmers [that] shared several languages… and communication [that] was mediated by local libraries, Franciscan and Catholic monasteries, schools and colleges, intellectual and religious organizations, presses and translations."[4]

A vast panorama of mid-nineteenth-century Banat, *Mara* is a chronicle of the region's multiethnic – Romanian, German, Hungarian, Serbian – social context, an interface of fiction and reality woven into one dramatic story that reflects the area's economic interests and decentralized multicultural traditions. Although shaped by ideological tensions and fundamental contradictions, the region developed powerful unifying and mediating forces over the centuries that countered segregation. Among such forces, Virgil Nemoianu identifies the Biedermeier cultural tradition, which combined "a timid Enlightenment with a vicarious Romanticism to produce contentment and confidence in the possibility and the actuality of progress" throughout nineteenth-century Central Eastern Europe. As an enormously powerful unifying element for all ethnic and religious groups, the Biedermeier culture of Banat "was informed by a broad acceptance of the values of family, throne, religion, privacy, learning, hard work, and tolerant coexistence."[5]

Told in the nostalgic tone of retrospective realism,[6] *Mara* takes place around 1850 when Banat, like neighboring Hungary, was under Austrian control but faced the political unrest of 1848-1849. A native of the region, Slavici portrays a world that incorporates and illustrates the values of a Biedermeier society and that adjusts to an ever expanding market economy and the dissolution of the idealized home as a solid anchor for social stability removed from the dangers of the outside world and its rampant materialism.

Hovering pleasantly between the urban and the rural, the novel's characters are motivated by such Biedermeier values as respectability, tradition, family stability, morality, labor, calm, learning, and steadiness. Illustrating the subordination of ethnic and linguistic differences to either economic pursuits or psychological interests, all the main characters of *Mara* belong to a society lacking a well-defined class structure and move freely among the large and small towns under Austrian control, from Lipova and Radna through Arad and Timişoara to Vienna or Budapest. In pursuit of advanced learning,[7] they frequent schools with varying linguistic or religious offerings and backgrounds. Guilds and traditional crafts still thrive; the rule of Austria's Habsburg dynasty is law-abiding and benevolent; and the pastoral comfort of hills and forests is never far away.

Beyond this idyllic world, *Mara* offers a reading of the female protagonists, Mara and her daughter Persida, as crucial in framing contradictions central to the tensions between traditional societies and the need to address female subjectivity as a matter at once immersed in the world and securely enclosed in its domestic core. Intertwined with the late nineteenth-century siege on the authority of the domestic sphere as an isolated space defined in opposition to the public world, the centrality of the feminine subject in *Mara* may well reflect the natural consequences of Slavici's awareness of the reevaluation of domesticity in the 1880s. As chief editor of the prestigious Romanian literary journal

*Vatra*, Slavici must have been familiar with the New Woman Movement of the 1890s that swept through the literary scene of Western Europe[8] and with its rendition of female subjectivity as mobile consciousnesses, defiant of conventional categories like propriety and domesticity.

Consolidating the novel's architectural construction with the narrative of a controversial courtship, *Mara* is also an account of the troubled love between Persida and Ignațius (Națl) Hubăr, the young son of a prosperous German family. After marrying in secret, Persida and Națl have a stormy and complicated relationship because of their parents' refusal to accept their love. After all, he is the son of well-to-do German parents, groomed to take over the prosperous family business; she is the daughter of Mara, petty trader and toll bridge collector, taken on charity at the convent by the compassionate Sister Aegidia, a tiny nun who is filled with pity at the sight of a pretty girl with unkempt hair and soiled clothes among the market crowds. Furthermore, Națl is Catholic and privileged, the only son of a Swabian[9] mother from Buda who dotes on him and of a Viennese father who is particularly influential in the Austrian-controlled community; Persida is Romanian Orthodox and presumably poor, the only daughter of a mother who feels that the German Madonna of the local Catholic church cannot perform miracles very well because no faith other than her own Orthodox religion is legitimate in God's eyes.

While reflecting the inability of tradition to recognize goodness outside itself, Persida's and Națl's marriage does not merely villainize tradition, it exposes their relationship in the domestic realm and calls upon the reader to decide what to think of the portraits of the mother and the daughter, Mara and Persida, two figures caught between the drive to destabilize conventions limiting women to confining roles and their cultural roles as bearers of a tradition that reflects their New Woman status in the familial position they inhabit. Both Mara and Persida have a fluid identity that allows them to add new dimensions to their socio-political subjectivity. Mapping new laws and expectations, the mother and the daughter give themselves new roles to assume and act out in the social economy of identities.

Thus Persida's marriage to Națl is an engaging process of give and take to construct her subjectivity, a process that occurs not only between Persida and Națl but also between Persida and Mara. In the union with Naţl, which hinges on the mechanisms of patriarchal power, Persida gives up an identity and simultaneously assumes another: that of Naţl's wife. In the eyes of her mother and community her identity as a Romanian Orthodox is exchanged for the socio-religious institutions of her German Catholic husband. Matrimony is thus the site of familial tensions and reflective of the rhythms of woman's initiatives, a situation calculated to show that Slavici does not idealize Biedermeier society and finds the power of the New Woman's intervention to be a driving force underlining a different, more gendered-balanced social stability.

*Mara*'s ample narrative scope is evident in the novel's two strains involving Mara and her children. The first is the "public" plot, which corresponds to social conventions and chronicles significant moments punctuating the social context that are skillfully interwoven with the accounts of interactions between Mara and her children, on the one hand, and the rest of the community, on the other. The second narrative strain focuses on the "private" plot, which corresponds to and contains the story of Mara's love for her children and her business transactions, her struggle to save money and her ambition to rise to prominence in the community, and her relationships with Trică and especially with Persida, who is romantically involved with Naţl, but also often likened to her mother when conducting her own business transactions.

The overall narrative action of *Mara* involves the gradual emergence of the private plot into the public sphere, and the overall conflict involves, beyond the clashes of the characters' personal needs and wants, an avalanche of ethnic tensions and turbulent contradictions caused by the progressive and more conservative strains of Biedermeier culture and its society. And only at the intersection of the public and private spheres does it become clear that, beyond capturing Mara's and Persida's essence as the story's protagonists, the novel illuminates realistic social and psychological detail corresponding to the most pressing contradictions emerging from ethnic, religious, and national conflicts, on the one hand, and from the challenges posed to a conventional society by the values and practices associated with a rising progressive bourgeois individualism and the emergence of new feminine values, on the other.

Slavici's emphasis on the depiction of Banat as a framework that embodies and expresses the large scope of the novel is clear from the beginning. An early chapter of the novel provides a memorable description of the country fair in the town of Arad, one of Banat's central towns, at which country folk bringing goods from seven surrounding regions come together in a jumbled collage:

> What an extraordinary event the autumn fair in Arad is!
>
> For weeks on end, the country roads are crowded with loaded carts, which bring the riches from seven regions to display them in the marketplaces and streets of Arad as well as the plains around it. And here gather carts crammed with fruit from the Criş and the Mureş valleys, lumber from the Abrud Mountains, and corn from the rich plains.
>
> There are rows of barrels filled with wine from the vineyards, as well as with brandy from the Mureş valley, flocks of sheep from Ardeal, herds of swine brought from the river meadows, stallions bred in the mountain clearings, and cattle driven by experienced traders.
>
> What a host of people and what a medley of garbs and languages! It seems as if here is the very middle of the world, where all humankind meets. At dusk, thousands of fires are lit around the town, by whose light people of all sorts talk or pass the time singing; here, Romanians, over there Hungarians, farther away Swabians or Serbians, in between them Slovaks and even Bulgarians. (52)

Although fragmentary and glancing, this description establishes the novel's framework as a metaphor of space that highlights the relational sites in which Mara and the other characters develop and express themselves. And it is in precisely these relational sites that shape Mara and her children where Slavici ultimately questions the endangered idyll upheld by the Biedermeier culture and the conventions of domestic life.

In the second half of the nineteenth century the Banat region witnessed a rise of individualism that rapidly began to transform society and labor. In the increasingly competitive industry of the area, individual effort became the means of material success. This was not only the era of the "self-made man" when the aristocratic privilege long held by the upper-classes could finally be challenged by individuals with talent, opportunity, and the capacity for simple hard work; it was also the time of the "self-made woman" whose values were shifting from domestic self-sacrifice and familial emotion to marketplace competitiveness and business-like rationality. The specter of material acquisitiveness, and thus less concern with parental responsibility than with higher profits, involved women like Mara in a particularly complex way. Bent on making money, she spends long hours at the market selling her product for a profit, while her children run around soiled and unkempt. Clever and shrewd, she peddles goods from one town to another and never returns home before selling all her merchandise:

> She'd sell whatever she could and buy whatever she could find. From Radna she'd take what you couldn't find in Lipova or in Arad; from Arad she'd bring back what you couldn't find in Radna or in Lipova. What mattered most for her was not to bring back what she had taken to market, and she'd rather sell with little gain than let her merchandise get moldy. (1)

Determined to succeed financially in spite of obvious hardships, Mara puts money aside every night in the three stockings she keeps – one for Persida, one for Trică and one for her own funeral. Her toughness and resilience recommend her as an early Mother Courage,[10] Bertolt Brecht's heroine with whom Mara seems to share more than a passing similarity. As in Brecht's play, the image of a preeminently courageous mother who tries to do best for her young hovers over Slavici's novel. Like Mother Courage, the itinerant trader who pulls her wagon of ashes containing her children, always preoccupied with her business of boots and brandy, Mara starts out as a petty trader and fierce single parent who soon becomes engaged in endless business transactions, from the selling of fish and vegetables at the town market, to taking on lease the bridge over the Mureş River to collect the toll, to selling lumber loaded onto rafts to merchants in Arad.

As for Mother Courage, business for Mara is but one of life's schemes by which she hopes to do well in spite of being an impoverished widow with two small children. The business transactions and her economical way of life are necessary, for they allow Mara to be in control of a life ultimately aiming to ensure public respectability and social advancement for her children.

Willing to put financial advancement above religious and ethnic xenophobia, Mara negotiates an advantageous arrangement with Sister Aegidia, the convent's treasurer, and sends Persida to the Catholic convent to be raised by the nuns (even though, like most Romanians, she is Orthodox). When Trică is expelled from school, Mara gives him as an apprentice to Steva Claici, a prosperous Serbian furrier from Arad. Mara's actions, which leave no doubt about her role as a transmitter of conventional values, impose control on her children's lives and reflect her attempt to fit the proper image of what she conceives her children should be and do. In moments of crisis, such as when Trică is expelled from school, Mara's ambitious plans for her children also reflect the Biedermeier values of her community: the belief in the innate equality of all people and in the social opportunity for self-betterment, and the unwavering confidence that learning and knowledge are supreme values:

> "Never mind, dear," she said to her son, steeling herself. "I'll find you a better school! I'll make you a man, a scholar, someone top-rank, so you won't be like your father or your mother, but will compel these peasants and their children to stand still in front of you, the way we have to now! I can. I have the means," she went on impetuously. "The Lord has given me and will continue doing so. He makes no distinctions between people." (9)

Mara's love for her children and the fierce pride she takes in them – she exclaims every so often that "Nobody has children like mine" – are matched by Mara's preoccupation with money. Convinced in an almost Calvinist fashion that money is evidence of a self-worth that "will raise you in your soul as much as in the eyes of others" (159), Mara tells Persida that "money is a great power, it opens all doors and breaks all laws" (147). Like Mother Courage, Mara's character advances the argument that money can be a moral force within society, finally triumphing over class pride, ethnic divisions, and institutional barriers. Her love of money and increasing greed make Mara's heart "laugh with delight" when on holy days worshippers come to the local church, St. Maria Radna, to pray to a miracle-working icon. It was not that Mara, a Romanian Orthodox, felt any divine grace, "For she did not believe that the icon could work wonders; she knew very well that a German Holy Mother was not a true Holy Mother." What really makes Mara's heart leap with joy is the knowledge that the gathered crowds were good for business:

> So it was all right that people should come to Maria Radna to worship, and Mara's heart would laugh with delight when, on Saint Mary's day, the fine weather would bring people from far and wide, from as far as a week's walk, in large crowds, their crosses adorned with flowers, carrying banners that waved in the wind, all singing psalms and litanies. When the hundreds and thousands gathered on the vast plain in front of the monastery, that day was Mara's harvest day; in the mornings she'd go out with full baskets and return in the evenings with empty ones. This is why Mara would pray in front of the icon, and then take her little ones, whom she always kept by her, push them a little ahead and say: "You pray too, mother's poor little ones!" (2)

Her unwillingness to part with her money is nowhere in the novel shown more poignantly than when she refuses to pay the ransom that would exempt her son Trică from military service. Unforgettable in her attempt to hold on to her money even when she knows that she is jeopardizing her son's life, Mara is again reminiscent of Mother Courage, whose son Swiss Cheese is in the end executed because she fails to put up the money required for his ransom. It's not that Mara does not love her son; like Mother Courage, she is not taking chances with her hard-earned money.

Above all, Mara's attachment to material gain and worldly ambition substitutes traditional domestic values and establishes the basis for a different claim that transcends moral authority. More importantly, Mara believes in a kind of inevitability combined with a degree of free will that prompts her to encourage Persida and Trică to cultivate self-assertion instead of self-denial, individual autonomy instead of the moral ambiguities of propriety, and an unbounded confidence in their own ability, talents, and rights.

This individualism is granted narrative and even moral authority by the very quality of the narration. At the level of the novel's action, Mara and her children enact the personal and social consequences of their epistemological relativism. In an early incident that sums up the complexities of individualism and highlights the problematic cohabitation of the region's differing ethnicities, languages, and religions, Trică, who has been beaten up at school by an older classmate left to supervise the pupils while the teacher went fishing, runs to Persida at the convent to ask for help in getting his revenge. When the two children, embarked upon their avenging mission, find themselves alone in a small boat tossed around by the swollen waters of the Mureş River, their mother, who is always at the end of the bridge collecting the toll, is the last to be worried about their safety. Always preoccupied with the community's perception of her children, and because she "knew that everything would run more smoothly if she kept a stiff upper lip," she rails at Sister Aegidia for having failed to keep Persida safe inside the convent, reproaching the nun with an accusatory, "All right, Sister, is this the way you take care of children?" (7)

As Persida's story – that she had no choice but to run and help her little brother beaten up by a classmate while the teacher, Mr. Blăguţă, had gone fishing – seems to absolve the children of the community's ire and reproach, Sister Aegidia openly condemns the teacher's lack of professional responsibility. But in doing so, the Catholic nun unwittingly instigates the ethnically mixed community against the Romanian teacher:

> "Behold," she said with solemn quiet, "instead of minding his classes he goes fishing, and meanwhile the children maim each other. How many other misfortunes could have occurred if it hadn't been for the Lord's care? No such things happen in our establishment!"
>
> "Sure," said Rosa, the wife of Hausler, the shoemaker across the street. "In our institutions there is law and order. With the Romanians, however, everything is topsy-turvy!"
>
> "That's true," a few said, while others laughed.
>
> This would have been all right if a few Romanians hadn't been there also; they blushed, either with anger or with shame.
>
> "I didn't mean it that way," said Sister Aegidia. "There is law and order among the Romanians, too, but it seems not everywhere."
>
> "This Blăguţă is a shame," added Mary, Ciondrea's wife; she couldn't stand the schoolmaster in Radna.
>
> Mara was fretting and fuming. She knew the Papists were inimical and she was very fond of Blăguţă, who was also a famous singer in the Romanian church. Then she also felt as if she had been pierced by a red-hot iron rod when she saw people and carts crossing the bridge without paying the toll. Anyway, the nun couldn't be right.

> "And how did my girl get out of the convent?" she asked,
> somehow uttering the words slowly. "Would it be by chance also
> our schoolmaster's fault if the children had drowned?"(7)

Finally, while the entire town is taking sides in the crisis that exposes the flaws in the Biedermeier formula for peaceful coexistence within this multiethnic region, Mara is secretly proud of her children's rebellious nature and daring behavior, indeed by their show of solidarity dictated by their love for each other. Their refusal to take a beating or to be disciplined when they believe that their rights and feelings are violated confirms Mara's steadfast belief that good people come only from "bad seed" and reveals that Trică and Persida are far from being sheltered within the confines of a domestic space and are instead exposed early on to the divisions and anxieties of the outside world.

In the developing narrative, Slavici uncovers the ideological complexities of such an upbringing by exploring the relationship between "duty" and feeling, between social norms and individual practices. Unwilling to be disciplined as a child but marked by the convent's rigid upbringing, Persida struggles later to contain her desire for Ignaţius Hubăr, which grows in spite of Mara's arguments – that marriage to Naţl was the wrong thing because he was of a different blood and that she would rather see Persida die than have her marry a German. When Persida hints that it might be God's will that she love Naţl, Mara bursts out:

> "No, no," Mara retorted with harsh determination, "this can't be!
> God knows," she went on, moved, "how much I've thought of
> you, how hard I've worked for you, how lovingly I've looked after
> you, and He can't punish me so cruelly. If I saw you dead, the
> entire joy of my life would be lost, but I'd tell myself that it has
> happened to other mothers as well and I'd find comfort in the end.
> But nobody in my family has ever defiled his blood!" she shouted,
> her eyes full of tears. "I, too, feel pity for him and for his mother,
> but you are dear to me and it can't be!" (p. 43)

The same Mara who sees fit to put her daughter in a Catholic convent for economic advancement strongly objects to her marriage into a prosperous German family since marriage would certify her identity as a Catholic through the subordinating institution of marriage. Thus Slavici makes clear that the domestic sphere is the most impervious to social change, ethnic amalgamation, and cultural integration. Social-climbing calls for putting aside religious and ethnic differences for material advancement, yet these differences are not always put aside, and it is in comparing the resilience of their prejudices that we find those aspects of society that are most opaque to cultural integration. Mara is willing to have her daughter educated in a Catholic convent, yet she opposes in the strongest possible terms her daughter's marriage into a prosperous German Catholic family. For all its force in shaping identity and thought, education does not compare to the social force that is marriage, which irrevocably alters Persida's religious and ethnic identity, and culminates in her decision to have her newborn son baptized Catholic.

Persida's love for Naţl becomes Slavici's vehicle to call for an examination of the inevitable confrontation between repressive social conventions and cultural legacy, on the one hand, and the desires of an individual heart, on the other. Romantic love, embodied in Persida's love for Naţl, is a primal emotion which is used in the novel as a counterpoint to the primal emotion of hatred, embodied by Mara. Since all the reasons why Persida and Naţl's love would be socially condemned are evident, Naţl's free-spirited friend Burdea absolves the lovers from the start as he decrees that "love is from another world and comes out of nowhere, you don't know how and it carries you away you don't know where" (73). Love, therefore, which has everything to do with a woman giving herself freely to the man she loves, allows Persida to become her own agency when she recognizes the imperatives of personal feelings.

The turning point in Persida's feelings occurs in the chapter XIV, "Bandi's Role." Before this chapter, Persida has maintained that she does not love Naţl, and thus the reader has remained engaged in the young woman's attempts to master her still active desire, not so much in the name of some authoritative principle but because circumstances – social reality – make such discipline necessary. In order for the critical shift in the narrative to take place, two things must happen: Persida must realize that she does indeed loves Naţl, and this recognition must be conveyed to the reader. Only then, with both lovers struggling to make social conventions express and accommodate their feelings, will the primary conflict shift the focus on romantic love, a convenient device whose delicate handling generates the surface tension and power of *Mara* while masking the social and cultural conflicts given prominence in the narrative.

In the beginning we cannot be sure of Persida's feelings. Raised by Sister Aegidia and aware of her mother's dislike of Naţl, Persida is mindful of the nun's views, namely that "this world isn't here for us to fulfill our hearts' desires, but to carry out our duties in it. First God, then your parents and, after them, all your benefactors" (38). Early on in the narrative, Naţl publicly embarrasses Persida, first at a wedding and then at a harvest celebration, and she seems determined to avoid him because she feels that he is reckless with his and her feelings both. Moreover, she is at this time courted by two other young men, Pavel Codreanu, a theologian, and Brădeanu, a lawyer. To her mother and brother, Persida insists that she is not in love with Naţl, but only feels sorry for him because he is despondent over his unrequited love for her. Soon, however, it becomes evident that in Naţl's grief Persida sees only a mirror image of her own lingering sorrow, and, in the comfort she tries to offer him, she sees only the medicine she has ineffectively administered to herself:

> "I have a soft spot for you, you know; you could see it and I, too, am telling you about it, since it is not my fault. It came like that, out of the blue, the way all misfortunes will. But this is all there is to it, and you can't know more than this. I took pity on you; but if you won't take pity on me, do whatever you please, for I, too, will do only what I want to!" (p. 38)

But contrasting Persida's public self-command with Naţl's demonstrative and eloquent suffering as he pursues her, we recognize how far Persida really is from indulging the pain she cannot help but feel. The incident involving Naţl in a nearly murderous fight with his father reduces Persida to her lowest emotional state. Subsequently, the young man's confession to her that he has in fact been wronged by his father, and not trying to murder him, shows Persida unequivocally that her love for Naţl is stronger than ever. When she is faced with her brother's harsh criticism of her passionate feelings, Persida speaks movingly of her love for Naţl:

> "I know," she went on excitedly, "that it was a misfortune for both of us that we saw each other, yet we still do. But my soul fills with unspeakable sweetness when I look into his eyes even if they are frowning, and I tremble whenever his hand touches me. It's not myself who wants it, nor does his will compel me, but an implacable fate that keeps us enthralled. The ground burns under my feet when I stay here with him secretly, and yet my true life is made up only of the moments spent with him. The rest is only struggling, consuming anxiety, hot desire." (99)

And even to Naţl's desperate plea that she must run away from him because he is a mere wretch who brings her and all those around him only bad luck, she replies calmly and self-assuredly:

> "No!" she finally said with quiet determination. "I will not be frightened away, I will not flee, I will not desert you!" she said, and caught his hand, clung to him and gently put her arm round his neck. "Oh," she went on as if in a dream, "how seductive is the thought that I will bring you out of the darkness you are lost in, brighten up your life, see you again...merry as you used to be once upon a time. I will get you out. I will brighten you up, you'll see. You will look at me and laugh the way you laughed when we met on the bridge. Ignaţius! Look at me!" she added, looking with stubbornness into his eyes.
> Laughing with tearful eyes, he was looking into her passionate eyes.
> Then, bending a little, he gently and shyly touched her temple with his lips, kissed her, and then moved her away from him. (93)

In Persida's moving plea, Slavici uses the most sophisticated version of romantic conventions to highlight the complexities raised by the clash of realistic social and psychological details within the Biedermeier society, on the one hand, and the failure of the domestic and monastic enclosures to regulate a New Woman's feminine instincts on the other.

The hardly accidental circumstance of Persida's and Naţl's meeting one stormy day when the wind breaks one of the convent's windows and, from across the street, the young man sees the beautiful Persida behind the shattered glass, makes clear that worldly influences penetrate even inside the space that ought to protect the girl but cannot. On the other hand, the ensuing *coup de foudre* highlights Persida as an aesthetic subject, all too open to the sensations of erotic love and pain (she suffers because she thinks that Naţl did not have the chance to see her well), and the peculiar affinities between them in the confines of a feminine sphere (the convent) that is tremblingly open to infiltration and dissolution from the outside world.

Persida's actions later on, when she decides to baptize her child as a Catholic, bring forward again the intersection of the spiritual and the worldly. The moment, marked by the interaction between the outside and the spiritual worlds as Persida and Naţl see each other through the shards of the broken convent window, comes full circle in the final baptism scene when Persida has her son baptized Catholic. So deeply has she been affected by her childhood spent at the convent that she is even more instrumental than her Catholic spouse in reinforcing the religious institution that breathes life into her married identity.

Coupled with the rise of individualism of the second half of the nineteenth century, such desires began to color the way in which personal happiness was conceptualized and pursued. As some scholars have argued,[10] fewer marriages were arranged by parents, and the choices of the heart encouraged young men and women alike to consider not only social compatibility and income, but also the affective intensity of romantic love as an essential component of courtship and marriage. In spite of the repeated warnings of clergymen and the religious establishment in general, and of alarmed parents in particular, about the dangers of unleashing individual desire and the risk of losing the protection and stability of traditional patriarchal society, young women like Persida began to recognize the imperatives of personal feelings and the relativity of ethical and epistemological values.

By bringing Persida's passionate love into public view, Slavici forces her to take the initiative, to act upon her own feelings and Naţl's desires. Just as her ministrations to Naţl have been in keeping with a young woman's proper behavior, so Persida's self-assertion at this point is gentle and selfless: acting only as opportunity allows, she becomes Naţl's bride in a secret ceremony performed at night by Codreanu, her former suitor who has become a village priest.

Since Mara has opposed all along Persida's marriage to Naţl, the conflict here is between the two central characters of the novel, Mara and Persida. Enacting the role of protagonist, Persida is driven by love whereas Mara, the antagonist, is driven by hatred. Since both women are acutely aware of the power of patriarchal institutions in shaping their destinies, both attempt to manipulate the institution of marriage in accordance with their desire. Driven by hatred, Mara refuses to grant Persida her blessing for the marriage to Naţl because she thus hopes to keep her daughter in her own worldview – that is with her blood unspoiled by a union with a German Catholic. (Giving her consent would simply mean that Mara would have to choose between her love for her daughter and her own strongly held xenophobia.) Countering her mother's hatred, Persida sees the marriage as the vehicle to overcome these religious and ethnic divisions, a view succinctly summed up in Lewis Hyde's observation that "marriage establishes a bond between clans and families, and, as part of an ongoing system of kinship, [the bride] becomes an agent of the community's cohesion and stability."[11]

Slavici highlights the crucial role marriage plays by having Persida's marriage blessed by her former suitor who is an Orthodox priest. In having Persida married by her former suitor, Slavici gives us a glimpse of an alternative future. Had Persida married Codreanu (an action fully embraced by Mara who goes as far as to discuss Persida's dowry with the go-between, Father Isai) she would have propagated the division. Having allowed her marriage to overcome the power of division, Persida becomes a fluid agent within the internal economy of identities. In this complex marketplace of shifting agencies her sexuality is the least significant aspect of her, as she faces the difficulty of confronting her mother, her husband and his family, and the community – in short, the outer economy of commodified human beings in the patriarchal world.

Even as Persida struggles to make social conventions accommodate her feelings, Naţl tries to do the same in the beginning. Together, they elope to Vienna where they are quite happy at first. But since neither Mara nor Naţl's parents have given their consent to the marriage, and since the priest who had secretly married them would be imprisoned if the news of a ceremony performed without parental consent were to be made public, the couple is forced to wait out while circumstances dictate their fate. Increasingly unhappy in Vienna,

Persida and Naţl return to Lipova, where Persida has to endure the shame of living outside social propriety.

After the couple buys the inn by the Sărărie, the inn and the tavern become a mystifying domestic space where Persida takes over the business and soon becomes more and more like her mother in the way in which she runs its operations. By anchoring Persida in this unusual, feminized space, Slavici poses the cultural problems of Persida's immersion in a compromising public realm. Her gradual change makes the case that Persida's appropriation of the tavern as feminized terrain threatens her aesthetic subjectivity and femininity:

> A woman worn out by backbreaking toil, she had gradually lost her fine and delicate appearance. As she kept heaving the heavy casks of water and the big pots from the fire, moving the tables from one place to another, lending a hand to everything, she had become sturdier, harder, but at the same time somewhat more knotty, like a tree which was still young but weather-beaten.
>
> Thus not even her movements remained the same as before. She walked more briskly, with bigger and heavier steps. She'd grab something with her whole palm and spin on her heels from one side to the other.
>
> By living permanently in touch with uneducated servants and people who gathered in the taverns, she had gradually lost the delicacy of her soul as well. She wasn't ashamed any more when she heard rude words, didn't feel hurt when spoken to harshly. She took the world as it was and her speech was fast, curt and rough — she could even slap or push when she had to have silence and order in her house. (117)

Persida's situation is especially cruel since, in spite of her devotion to him, she is psychologically abused and often beaten by Naţl, who treats her contemptuously and openly questions the validity of their marriage. Having promised a family friend to get rid of Persida in order to free himself and to make his mother happy, Naţl appears ready to succumb to religious and ethnic pressures by publicly invalidating his marriage to Persida. All along Mara treats her daughter as an outcast and, whenever Persida is beaten up, she cherishes the thought that in the end she "will leave the German." In the meantime, Persida's newly acquired identity as uncontested mistress of the inn at the Sărărie causes more than an undulating ripple in the community. As the inn begins to be known as "Persida's place," Persida triggers a principle of complimentarity and a binary unity between her and Naţl. Moving beyond Naţl's shadow, she functions in turn as a signifier of her own womanly agency by nourishing the hope of becoming a mother.

Having used the institution of marriage to counter her mother's opposition to her love for Naţl, she is now ready to manipulate motherhood to rein in Naţl, who spends his time drinking and playing cards with friends. His violent and disorderly life stems early on from the tension between the conservative and the progressive strains of the Biedermeier culture, played out in the narrative context of the novel by the generational conflict between Naţl and his father, Anton Hubăr. Having denied his son the opportunity to continue his studies, the master butcher had also pressured Naţl to take over the family, business because "My father was a butcher as well, so was his father and all in our kin were butchers ever since we've known ourselves." Further complicating the already strained father-son relationship is the inescapable ghost of the father's adulterous relationship with a poor Hungarian servant, Reghina, who had given birth to the illegitimate and emotionally handicapped Bandi. Taken in out of pity at Persida and Naţl's tavern, the homeless Bandi is the only Hungarian whom Naţl, who hated Hungarians, could tolerate around him. Old Hubăr's murder in the last chapter of the novel when Bandi's paternity is revealed, comes as a shocking and confusing ending which offers few clues for the reader's full understanding of the narrative plot.

Beyond that crippling resolution, however, Slavici's energetic intentionality is rich and engaging in the depictions of Mara and Persida as New Women whose claims to their new identity are solidified by the opposing male characters, Anton Hubăr and Naţl. For even though the still-prosperous guilds and patriarchal structure seem to preserve a vanishing type of the old culture, the rise of a modern competitor like Mara, and also Persida, the new mother and businesswoman, show the robust signs of modernization. Altering the domestic sphere's definition by challenging its distance from a compromised public world, Mara's and Persida's stories are consonant with a modern, woman-centered culture. Their shrewd ability to attain financial success and to manipulate an obsolete social structure attracts the admiration of such pillars of the old community as the town treasurer and the master-butcher Anton Hubăr. When Mara offers more money than he does as a gift for Persida's and Naţl's newborn son, Hubăr looks at her in amazement, "as she was just a helpless woman." He also feels "like crying every time he looked at Mara's serene face" during the great feast celebrating Trică's and Naţl's acceptance as masters into the furriers' guild. Defiant and victorious, she is the reigning spirit of the large gathering which seems to encapsulate a modified domestic sphere:

> With the conviction that it had been she who'd brought them together and that her own children represented the knot that kept them tight, she walked around proudly and lightly, as if she had wings, and spoke slowly and emphatically like an empress. (162)

In similar fashion, Naţl barely seems to live up to those obligations which Persida fulfilled before the birth of her son. Left to take care of the Sărărie, he "was up all day long, kept in constant motion, argued with the servants and with the people in the tavern. Only now did he realize how Persida had been spending her life while he talked to friends, took long walks or killed time gambling" (157).

The symbolism and values attached to masculinity and femininity seem to undergo profound transformations. Far from being perceived through Hubăr's or Naţl's consciousness and represented as objects, Mara and Persida defy the static mystery of a traditional fictional portrait and resist definition as specifically gendered. Their active presence speaks of a dynamic self, which seems to pose a challenge to traditional domesticity. In the vein of the New Woman, they are representative examples of a universal category that provides a general model and announces liminality and universality as opposed to marginality and domesticity in the functions and roles of women in fiction and in society.

### Notes

1. Alexandru Piru, *Istoria Literaturii Române*, Editura Grai şi Suflet, (Bucureşti: Cultura Naţională, 1994), 104-5.

2. The Banat region came successively under Turkish (1552-1718), Austrian (1718-1867) and Dual Monarchy (i.e., Austro-Hungarian) control (1867-1919) before becoming part of Romania in 1919.

3. Victor Newman, *Tentaţia lui homo-europaeus: Geneza spiritului modern in*

*Europa centrală şi de sud-est*, (Bucureşti: Editura ştiinţifică, 1991). English translation: *The Temptation of Homo Europaeus*, trans. Dana Miu (Boulder and New York: East European Monographs/Columbia University Press, 1993).

4. Marcel Corniş-Pope, "Literary and Cultural Production in a Marginocentric Cultural Node: The Case of Timişoara," forthcoming in *A History of the Literary Cultures of East-Central Europe: Conjunctions and Disjunctions in the 19th and 20th Centuries*, (New York and Amsterdam: John Benjamin Press), 2003/2004.

5. Virgil Nemoianu, "Biedermeier Cultural Intertextuality in Transylvania: The Case of Ioan Slavici," in *The Comparatist: Journal of the Southern Comparative Association* XVI (1992): 62-69.

6. Used in such novels as George Eliot's *Middlemarch*, several of Balzac's novels, or Thomas Mann's *Buddenbrooks*, this kind of realism seems to derive from a modified historical novel and establishes an epic distance of about forty to fifty years between the writing present and the time of the narrative.

7. For an informative discussion of the "learning ethos" in the Banat region of that period, see Virgil Nemoianu's "Learning over Class: The Case of the Central European Ethos" in *Cultural Participation: Trends since the Middle Ages*, eds. Ann Rigney and Douwe Fokkema (Amsterdam: John Benjamins, 1993), 79-107.

8. Of the writings of the period, mention must be made of the best-known New Woman writer George Egerton's 1893 collection of short stories *Keynotes* and Sarah Grand's article "The New Aspect of the Woman Questions." Both focus paradoxically on female subjectivity as disrupting convention in general and conventional marriage in particular.

9. The two distinct German communities of Transylvania were the Protestant and somewhat patrician German Saxons of the southern area and the Catholic Swabians of the Banat in the southwestern part.

10. The similarities between Slavici's *Mara* and Brecht's *Mother Courage* have never been explored. *Mara* was translated into German in 1960, almost two decades after the first staging of Brecht's play, so the playwright's contact with Slavici's text is unlikely. On the other hand, however, Brecht's wife and muse was Viennese, and Slavici was a well-known author around the time when she was growing up in the Austrian capital where Slavici himself had spent a formative period of his life.

11. Lewis Hyde, *The Gift: The Imagination and the Erotic Life of Property*, (New York: Vintage, 1979).

12. One scholar who has so argued is Lawrence Stone, in *The Family, Sex and Marriage in England 1500-1800* (New York: Harper and Row, 1977).

# Male Boundaries and Feminine Spaces:
# The Ideal Community of Mihail Sadoveanu's
# *Tales from Ancuța's Inn*

A small masterpiece made up of nine tales heard by a nameless narrator at a roadside inn in Moldavia,[1] Mihail Sadoveanu's *Tales from Ancuța's Inn* brings together a community represented by a group of story-telling travelers. Although the framing of this narrative is similar to that of Chaucer's *The Canterbury Tales*, the assembled company and the stories they tell evoke a sense of the social, moral and spiritual values of the Romanian community within a specific historical context, with the inn representing an imaginary construction, an ideal setting for story-telling contests, but also a symbolic space in the narrative formation of national identity. Commodified as national stereotypes, the travelers who stop at Ancuța's Inn to tell stories draw from the whole range of the mid-nineteenth-century Moldavian community and use this Romanian eastern province as an irradiating background space. A reclusive shepherd, a secretive monk, a worldly merchant, a shrewd water witch, a well-traveled blind beggar, an affable freeman, a melancholy one-eyed captain, and a wise astrologer drink new wine from old mugs, feast on roasted chicken smeared with garlic, and tell stories that feature the *raconteurs* as principled upholders of the social order. And Ancuța's Inn momentarily becomes the space balancing the clamor of historical past (the days of Moldavia's rulers and their turbulent times) with the sound of the travelers' voices and the poised instant of their cultural fusion, not by rational cognition but by the redeemed mystery of the shared heritage connoted in their stories.

Presiding over the story-telling is the beautiful innkeeper Ancuța whose natural freedom as heir to her mother's inn keeping business and as a prosperous businesswoman in her own right warrants her autonomy from the male-dominated social and narrative order. For even though the self-legitimizing discourse of the anonymous male narrator, who benefits from a position of authority conferred on him by his gender and class, relates the order and appearance of the storytellers,

Ancuţa is the one at ease with the intersections of the outer worldly inn and with her central presence in its space. Empowered as a generator of male homosocial bonding, she is the reigning spirit of the travelers' gathering, and she seems to supervise, through her inherited right of ownership over the inn, a modified domestic sphere: the ideal community that is the nation. In greeting her customers, Ancuţa reveals an underlying determination to define through their presence the community's ethnic identity and mark spatial boundaries. Her inn is located in lower Moldavia, at the crossroads of well-traveled paths leading to the crowded marketplaces of scattered towns, paths leading all the way up north to the border with Russia, the country of "the White Emperor and his Muscovites."[2] More importantly, Ancuţa ensures compatibility or harmony between the sophisticated narrator, who possesses an unruffled sense of superiority in status and performance, and the travelers, who legitimize a vibrant and pluridimensional world anchored in old customs and cultural patterns.

As in the outside world of the Romanian community at large, all the characters' allocation of space and roles seems pretty fixed at the inn. Their community carries the connotations of ethnicity and recommends itself as an ideal community, which exhibits what Derrida calls a logic of identity.[3] This consists of the small group's desire to frame ideas together in a unity of consciousness, to define a social and cultural identity as a whole, and to form a closed totality with borders firmly drawn. Relying on the illusion of pure present, the travelers conceive the being and truth of things as lying outside time and change. They also have a constitutive conception of self as the product of an identity it shares with others, all of whom mutually understand and affirm one another.

What is most evident in the very formation of the idea of the *Tales* is its compositional order and regularity. The principle of ordered composition underlies a complete narrative range – from witty, bordering on bawdy tales like "The Prince's Mare" to the dramatic tone of the monk's story relating the tragic end of the great robber Haralamb; from the elfish naughtiness of the young bride Irinuţa in "The Dragon" to the tragic love story told by Captain Isac in "The Well Among the Poplars"; from the violence and eroticism of "The Other Ancuţa" to the unspeakable cruelty against a wronged husband in "Justice of the Poor"; and from the wonder of faraway lands brought among the storytellers at the inn by the traveling merchant Cristişor Dămian to a different kind of fantastic revealed in the tales of the blind beggar and of Zaharia the Water Witch.

Beyond distinctions of class, literacy and comprehension between the travelers and the sophisticated narrator, the reader of the *Tales* is invited to share in a common perspective as a fellow observer of the human race in a particular cultural space. The systematic praise of moral worth evident in the way the travelers' address one another does more than determine the reader's perception of the tales they tell; it effectively weaves the moral and social fabric of the world to which they belong. Representing Moldavia's normative social class of that period, that of the freemen, is one traveler whom the others, observing the dictates of social hierarchy, respectfully call "worthy *Comis*."4 By introducing the *Comis* early on in the narrative, the unnamed narrator of the *Tales* cleverly uses him to offer a detailed account of the interactions at the inn and to familiarize the reader with the small-group community of travelers stopping at Ancuţa's Inn:

> Standing there like a pillar, in those fat and happy days, was a freeman from elsewhere, and he was very dear to me. He would raise his mug to everyone, listen to the songs of the Gypsy musicians with a far-away look in his eyes.... He was a tall, grey-haired man with a wizened and deeply wrinkled face. His skin was etched with innumerable small creases around his close-cropped mustache and his small eyes. His eyes were passionate and misty. His face, with its short mustache, seemed to smile sadly.
>
> His name was *Comis* Ioniţă. Now this *Comis* Ioniţă had a fairly fat purse on his belt, under his coarse, grey clothes, and he had come to the inn mounted on a horse. (20-21)

The scope of the travelers' journey, which in four of the tales is a pilgrimage to the Church of Trei Ierarhi in Iaşi, Moldavia's capital, attests to a shared sense of purpose and faith for the entire gathering as it brings into the narrative the image of one of the region's architectural gems. Built during the reign of the Moldavian ruler Vasile Lupu, the Church of Trei Ierarhi incorporates a variety of styles in its construction – Turkish, Arabic, Georgian, Armenian and Persian, among others – and thus signifies Moldavia's cultural prominence as far back as the early seventeenth century.5 More importantly, as the travelers' stated destination, the Church of Trei Ierarhi is an overt manifestation of God's presence, and thus a stabilizing factor in the life of this Christian community, as well as a subtle reminder to the reader that an understanding of the *Tales* requires a moral and spiritual consensus at once Romanian and Orthodox in the interpretation of the text.

Sincerity of religious belief, which demands a lack of cynicism; assurance of social status, doubled by a social ease that requires tolerance as well as success; and a love of the society of one's fellow men and women, coupled with a generous estimate of the possibilities of human nature, sum up the spirit of the travelers and are all to be cultivated in order to experience the unity of Sadoveanu's real and imagined worlds.

If the reader understand the completeness of the nine stories and masterful transparency of the *Tales'* design in this light, to appreciate the nine stories even further he must consider the elements of Sadoveanu's universe in their due order – social, moral, and spiritual.

As in *The Canterbury Tales*, the structuring of the narrative in terms of portraits satisfies a pre-modern set of aesthetic expectations suited to the time of the narratives: like wall paintings, carvings, and statues set in niches on the outside of great buildings, the travelers at the inn direct the reader's gaze outward to the created world (of which he comes to form a part) and not inward to the individual psyche. The unity of the *Tales* is built upon the assembled company of travelers, with the narrator actually a part of the social order that he describes and a means for the reader of entry into it. Once inside, the reader can easily recognize each of the travelers at the inn from the meticulous, two-tiered description which relates to their countenance and identifiable attire: the Merchant who "wore a fur cap and coat and [whose] beard was tidy, neatly cut and rounded with scissors. He was beaming all over his full and jovial face – the face of a man who had always eaten plentifully" (91); the blind beggar, "with his expressionless face, framed in its wild beard, [and] dressed like a mountain-dweller, with a little black hat, the white costume of his people, and a sheepskin cloak clasped only at the shoulder" (103); or the unforgettable Captain Isac "with a swarthy face, a short mustache and a rounded beard, an aquiline nose and dark eyebrows that still held the traces of manly beauty, although his right cheek was crumpled under the dry eye-socket permanently set in a mask of agony, while his live eye, large and dark, merely stared down into the black well of the past; he wore high boots of Russian leather and a tunic of blue woolen cloth with round silver buttons, held at this side a yellow leather bag, and there were pistols in his holster" (48-9).

In terms of their class and trade, the travelers belong to Moldavia's agrarian society of the second half of the nineteenth century, which is also the predominant time period of the tales told at Ancuța's Inn. As a cohesive social group, the travelers are both humble and prosperous peasants, vintners, carters, shepherds, and even beggars, with distinct values and aspirations that set them apart from the upper class of the *boieri*.[6] But even though they are different from one another, their constitutive concept of self is expressed by the concept of the community to which they belong. As Michael Sandel argues in a different context, their

> constitutive self-understandings comprehend a wider subject than the individual alone, whether a family, a tribe or a city or class or nation or people, to the extent [that] they define a community in the constitutive sense. And what marks such a community is not merely a spirit of benevolence, or the prevalence of communitarian values, or even certain 'shared final ends' alone, but a common vocabulary of discourse and a background of implicit practices and understandings within which the opacity of persons is reduced, if never finally dissolved.[7]

At Ancuţa's Inn, the travelers become fused and mutually sympathetic, and they understand one another as they understand themselves. Thus in Sadoveanu's ideal community, the travelers stopping at Ancuţa's Inn appear not as separated but rather as shared selves, connected by a logical dependency as a prevailing condition of their society. They are the ones best able to judge occurrences from the past and to become alarmed at the prospect of a threat to social harmony and well being.[8] It is there, in their midst, that the terms of inclusion or exclusion are formulated, with the tales acting as an argument and criteria for the selection process. Stories of inclusiveness take account of persecuted lovers (the young *mazâl* and Aglăiţa, the *boier*'s daughter in "The Tale of Zaharia the Water Witch," or the bold Todiriţă Cătană and the Lady Varvara in "The Other Ancuţa") and of outlaws who defend the lowly and the helpless (like the thief Vasile the Great and the suffering peasant in "Justice of the Poor"). Other tales argue for the exclusion of evil rulers like Duca-Vodă ("The Blind Beggar's Tale"), cruel and greedy high ranking officials like Costea Căruntu ("The Other Ancuţa"), wicked and depraved *boieri* like Răducan Chioru ("Justice of the Poor") or Năstase Bolomir ("The Dragon"), and heartless gypsies like Hasanache who murder their own for immediate gain ("The Well Among the Poplars").

And since a human identity is more truly moral than social, Sadoveanu attaches greater significance to the moral than the social identity of the travelers. They are people of proven moral excellence and worthy of admiration, men of faith and honest laborers, who offer an optimistic view of the soundness of society as a whole. Honorable and courteous with each other, the travelers seem perfected by the habit of virtuous living, and their honesty shields them against material acquisitiveness.

But although the possibility of a virtuous life is firmly upheld and asserted at all levels of society, the very setting of the stories – the inn with its wine drinking and revelry and with Ancuţa swinging her hips in front of Captain Isac – impresses upon us from the outset the ineradicable fact of human frivolity, and even sinfulness. Several of the tales, such as "The Monk's Tale," "The Blind Beggar's Tale," and "The Merchant's Tale," are told by travelers going on a pilgrimage to a church, as the protagonists prepare to answer to God for what they have done with their lives. "The Tale of Haralamb," for instance, does not overlook human imperfection but rather constructs the whole narrative within that context. A good man, the storyteller's father, becomes a thief and ends up being hunted down like an animal by his own brother, Captain Gheorghie. Now an adult and a monk, the storyteller reveals that his mother had promised him to God, and thus we are gently re-minded not only of the father's crimes but also of the son's illegitimacy and of the need to expiate for both of his parents' sins. Beyond our tol-erance of ordinary human sins and foibles and follies, absolutions are not matters to be trifled with. The travelers' purpose in going to offer penance is imaginatively convincing because it is a part of the very fabric of their society, which the narrative reveals.

Beyond these stories, the *Tales* situates the inn as another un-forgettable and extraordinary space in Romanian literature. It is suffi-cient to mention in this context Ioan Slavici's novella *Moara cu Noroc* (The Lucky Mill), in which the inn becomes an evil space of bloody encounters, horrid crimes, and broken lives, or Ion Luca Caragiale's *Mânjoală's Inn*, which shelters illicit erotic games used as a complex and complicated narrative circuit to unravel an oppressive patriarchal structure.[9] Charged with symbolic connotations, the inn is also a memorable presence in other works by Sadoveanu, such as *Moş Precu's Tavern* (1904) and *Nicoară Potcoavă* (1952). Summing up its important role in the *Tales,* Teodor Vârgolici considers the inn "a specific component of the structure of the Romanian nation."[10]

Vârgolici's commentary is so relevant in any discussion of the *Tales* that it deserves further scrutiny. In a short note that precedes the

1964 edition of the *Tales*, Sadoveanu complicates the issue of the inn's authenticity by bringing his own childhood memories into the discussion. Declaring that his own mother had spent her childhood in the region around the inn "in a poor little village called Verşeni," and that he himself had seen it as a child whenever he went to visit his grandparents, Sadoveanu proclaims categorically that

> Ancuţa's Inn is no fiction. It actually existed and was famous in the past century. Its ruined walls still stood some ten years ago when the last heirs divided the bricks to build two modest farm houses for themselves, not very distant from each other.[11]

First seen with the eye, in the visual transfer arising between writer and reader the inn can then be appropriated as a text. And since seeing as reading clearly involves a metaphorical construct, the inn becomes the frame for the story as well as a narrative space. In this latter capacity, however, Ancuţa's Inn has the cultural dimension of a sacred space, in which tradition and history are articulated simultaneously while they legitimize the Romanian community as a nation. Poised in this metaphorical stasis between past and future, the inn also entails a language metaphor in which two functions are fulfilled: it can be recognized as falling within a class of literary tropes well established in Romanian literature; and it connotes a significant place embedded in the text that is understandable through a literary typology reinforced in a cultural and social context. This type of metaphorical construct advances, in turn, a circular thinking, by which the inn forms a united image, a fusion of culture and history but also an architectural structure with its own symbolic associations that allow for literary interpretations.

From the start, the narrator states that

> Ancuţa's Inn was not merely an inn, but a genuine fortress. It had walls as thick as from here to way over there, and barred gates such as I've never seen in my life. People, cattle, and carts could take shelter within and be without fear of the thieves and robbers.
>
> At the time I'm speaking of there was still peace in the land and good will amongst men. The gates of the inn stood wide open like those at the Prince's court. And on mild autumn days you could see the Moldova Valley through them, stretching as far as

the eye could see, and the mountain mists on the evergreen forests
as far away as Ceahlău and Hălăuca.[12] And, when the sun buried
itself in the other world and the distant landscape dimmed and slid
into dark mystery, the fires in the courtyard lighted up the stone
walls, the dark recesses of the doors and the latticed windows.
Then the musicians' songs would cease for a while and the stories
begin. (20)

With its thick walls the inn, one might say, represents the body of
a man. It is rigid and symmetrical, muscular and protected with barred
gates which look like armor. The combination of the geometry, the
phallic imagery, and the way in which the building looks like a man in
armor is intimidating and is meant to be so. The whole structure dominates a large court constructed with little regard for what had been on
the site. It marks its triumph with the high gates that send out travelers
across the Moldavian land. But while this outside geometry of stone
walls marks a cold and intimidating place, the inside of the inn, which
is the innkeeper Ancuța's realm, is a domesticated space. Here people
are drifting in and out, wine and food are served continuously, and men
gather to tell stories associated with the narration of small-scale epics
or factual events, past or present. The oldest of the travelers stopping at
the inn, the astrologer *Moş* Leonte,[13] gives the following account:

> Ever since I could remember, from the time of the Ancuța of the
> past, we, in these parts, have been used to sitting and talking
> things over, paying homage to the wine of the South at the same
> time. And while enjoying this most excellent drink, we listen to
> stories of the past. In my opinion,…there isn't another inn like this
> to be found anywhere, no matter how much you'd wonder the
> Earth. Such fortress-like walls, such barred windows, such cellars
> – such wine! Can they be found anywhere else? They cannot! Nor
> can such sweetness, such high spirits nor such dark eyes. I'd be
> content to live under their spell until the time comes to moor my
> boat to the shore that no storm ravages. There's no need for you to
> knit your brows, Mistress Ancuța, for I was a friend of your
> mother's. And I read her future in my almanac, just as I did yours.
> (36-37)

Ancuța's Inn is thus also a picture of the relationship between men
and women in the Moldavian community of the time. Men dominate

and rule over the public space as they drink wine and tell their stories, yet women like Ancuța have their revenge. Nobody really cares about the inn's architecture, and most people who stop at the inn don't even notice its shape which men have erected. It is inside the inn where Ancuța pours the wine and "stirs the fire smoldering under the ashes" (48) that one can find a place where reality and fantasy mix and where fine food, good wine, and good cheer welcome the travelers. The inn is thus Ancuța's temple where she cooks and cleans, and where she has her role to play: she makes livable and enjoyable the interior realm, the inside space which is warm, sheltering and comfortable.

But she really does more than that. The story *The Other Ancuța*, which is the fifth and central narrative among the nine stories, does not only introduce the other Ancuța, the younger innkeeper's mother, as a woman-subject within the story itself. It also highlights her role in devising a clever escape for the bold Todiriță Cătană and his love, Lady Varvara, and her symbolic status consonant with a modern woman-centered reinterpretation of Romanian culture. In helping the two lovers, who come from opposing social classes, the other Ancuța uses her intellectual prowess to manipulate a patriarchal structure and to attain societal change through social disintegration: with the two lovers' escape and subsequent marriage, love turns into a powerful weapon, a place of passage or a threshold where nature confronts a rigidly categorizing culture. A site for the transformation of the social power relations, the space of the inn where Todiriță Cătană seeks shelter becomes a ferociously feminine place. Here the other Ancuța humbles the power structure and reinscribes the traditional roles of men and women in a changing society.

Drawing on folk stories that stem from a collective past and portray iconographic characters, the stories told at the inn form a homogenized amalgam, an imagined community that corresponds to Herder's notion of *Volk* and is analogous to the process of nation-building through myth-making and fabulation. In this context, the sorrowful tune of the *Miorița* ballad played by the traveling blind beggar on his bagpipes has a special significance. As a cultural testament of a people's national identity, the ballad is the property of every Romanian from the historically divided provinces, represented in the ballad's verses by the three shepherd-protagonists: one is a Moldavian, the other a Wallachian (Vrancean), and the third a Transylvanian (Ungurean).[14]

While accommodating regionally specific accounts, the different versions of the *Miorița* retain common narrative elements – especially in the minimal action plot and the psychological representation of the murdered shepherd's passive attitude towards his own death – as well as certain symbolic attributes and characteristics of Romanian morality, philosophy and artistic sensibility that allow a cross-cultural recognition of the tale in all Romanian communities.[15] As a testimony to the ballad's strong cultural appeal, when the blind beggar sings the *Miorița*, all the travelers at the inn listen in rapture to its melancholy tune, which is to them a moving emotional experience and one that is renewed with every chance they get to hear it.

Since, as Benedict Anderson has pointed out, European nations were created around well-known myths and legends like those of Roland, Boadicea, Vercingetorix, etc., the narratives told in the *Tales*, like the *Miorița* ballad, stem from a narrative consciousness which in turn confers a sociological solidity upon the iconographic characters of the *Tales*.[16] Each of the storytellers seeking shelter and merriment at Ancuţa's Inn portrays in turn a protagonist firmly entrenched in a specific social milieu – a village, a small town, the Prince's court, etc. – that provides an analogous construct for both the narrative world of the inn and its symbolic space. In the ideal, face-to-face community of the inn that signifies the nation, there is mutual understanding, group identification, and cultural loyalty.

But although the narrative matrix of the stories presents a veritable *tour d'horizon* in which the travelers interact in a plurality of contexts proposed as the ongoing principle of the whole of Romanian society, it does not offer *un tour du monde*. The stories are precisely delineated and, in spite of the differences in tone and narrative register, they affirm an ethnically and culturally identifiable space and a collective portrait of the Romanian community. Recognizing the specific value of face-to-face interactions and small-group relations, the Merchant's tale, for example, advances the appreciation of specialties of Romanian cuisine, such as devilled lamb in garlic paste, sour soup, and sarmale, only to stir the other travelers' delight in adopting such delicacies as their own favorites. Insofar as they see themselves as a group that shares a specific heritage and set of cultural norms, the travelers also fear oppositional differentiations. Their horror at the things the Merchant has seen in foreign lands, from trains defined as "rows of little houses on wheels that fit on to iron rails" to "streets made of one piece of stone" and "ladies with hats and gentlemen with watches" (96), identify the travelers at the inn as a homogenous group, with common attributes and a similar point of view of the world.

In this sense, the *Tales* reaffirms the notion that, beyond political and economic considerations, a nation recommends itself through processes of common culture and common self-identification that hold a people together and enable it to survive in spite of outside danger and political disintegration. Identifying themselves with the Romanian people, the travelers at the inn use in their stories a performative discourse that critics like Regis Debray[17] recognize as forming the basis of the will to nationhood.

Similarly, the descriptive passages of the *Tales* suggest an atemporal universe that defies chronology and generational barriers to champion the national ethos. In the presence of Ancuţa the Younger, who is the spitting image of her mother and who duplicates in her reaction to the narrated stories her mother's actions, the past captures the present in a genealogy that mirrors the will to nationhood suggested from the beginning of the *Tales*:

> One golden autumn I heard many a tale at Ancuţa's Inn. But that was long ago, during the year in which such awful rains fell on St. Elijah's Day that people said that they had seen a black dragon up in the clouds over the overflowing water of the Moldova River. They also saw some birds, the like of which had never before been seen, whirl in the storm and sail towards the East. And *Moş* Leonte, consulting his almanac and explaining the signs of Emperor Heraclitus, showed that these birds, whose feathers were the color of frost, had been borne hither by the winds that rose from the islands at the edge of the Earth and foretold war between Empires, as well as an abundant grape harvest.
>
> And the White Emperor did indeed throw his Muscovites against the pagan world, and, that the stars should fulfill their prophecies, God gave such abundant crops to the vineyards of Lower Moldavia that the vintners didn't have enough barrels for their wine, and the carters from our parts set out to bring the wine to the mountains. Then came the time for revelry and story-telling at Ancuţa's Inn.

Convoys of carts rumbled along outside incessantly. The folk
musicians played and sang inside ceaselessly. Whenever one of the
musicians would collapse from exhaustion and wine another would
jump up and take his place.

And the men drinking smashed so many mugs and jugs that, for
two years afterwards, women crossed themselves while passing the
inn on their way to the marketplace at Roman.[18] And, at the fires,
tried and true masters roasted choice cuts of ram and veal, or grilled
fish fresh from the Moldova River. (19)

More than any other of Sadoveanu's works, the *Tales* communi-
cates the continuity of tradition in the national memory and allows for
liberating forms of cultural identification. It is through the nationalized
space of an ideal community which consistently asserts the subordination of individual aims and values to the collective ethos that the
homogenizing myths of the stories being told at Ancuţa's Inn relate the
nation's unifying narrative. Ultimately, the transcended synthesis of an
ideal community, in which opposites and differences are reconciled and
balanced, and individuality, which rests on the unity of general will and
individual subjectivity, generates the nation.

### *Notes*

1. Moldavia, the eastern province of modern Romania which is used as background for
all the stories in *Tales from Ancuţa's Inn*, was an independent territory under the rule of a
Voivod or Prince until 1859, when it was reunited with the southern territory of Wallachia to
form the Romanian state. Historically, this province which covered the area along the eastern
Carpathians bordering the Danube and the Black Sea to the south and the Dniester River to
the north, was brought to prominence and consolidated as an independent state in the early
fourteenth century during the reign of Alexander the Good. Throughout its turbulent history,
Moldavia had to fight against the frequent invasions of the Tartars and of the Turks.

2. All quotations are from *Tales from Ancuţa's Inn* (Bucharest: Editura Institutului
Cultural Român, 2004), 19. The *Tales* will be the shortened form of the novel's full title by
which I will identify *Tales from Ancuţa's Inn* in this chapter.

3. Jacques Derrida, *Of Grammatology* (Baltimore: Johns Hopkins University Press,
1976), 12-87.

4. The *Comis* was a ranking official in Moldavia similar to an equerry, and whose
position corresponded to that of a squire. Such a person was usually chosen from among the
freemen, or free landholders, called *răzăşi*.

5. Built between 1637-1639, the Church of Trei Ierarhi was initially a monastery
erected during the reign of Vasile Lupu. The three saints in whose honor the church was
named – Vasile Cel Mare, Ioan Gura de Aur and Grigore of Nazianz – are all from the
fourth-century Cappadochian region. One of the most frequently visited churches in Roma-

nia, this beautiful construction that includes thirty different decorative styles is also the site of the tombs some of Moldavia's most prominent rulers, such as Dimitrie Cantemir (1710-1711) and Alexandru Ioan Cuza (1859-1866), the first monarch of the united Romanian provinces of Wallachia and Moldavia.

6. *Boieri* were members of the landed gentry in the Romanian provinces of Moldavia and Wallachia. This title should not to be confused with *boyard*, a privileged aristocratic order abolished by Peter the Great in Russia around 1591.

7. Michael Sandel, *Liberalism and the Limits of Justice* (Cambridge: Cambridge University Press, 1982), 172-73.

8. While she does not specifically speak of her ideal community, Seyla Benhabib expresses a similar ideal of person relating to one another through reciprocal recognition of subjectivities in what she calls the "standpoint of the generalized other," which abstracts from the difference, desires and feelings among persons, to regard all as sharing a common set of formal rights and duties. See Seyla Benhabib, "The Generalized and Concrete Other: Toward a Feminist Critique of Substitutionalist Universalism," *Praxis International* 5, no. 4, (1986), 402-24.

9. For a detailed discussion of these works see my book *Silent Bodies: (Re)Discovering the Women of Romanian Short Fiction* (Boulder and New York: East European Monographs/Columbia University Press 2002).

10. "Postfața la *Hanu Ancuței*," București: Editura 100+1, GRAMAR (2001), 117-122.

11. This note, which is included in this English translation of *Tales from Ancuța's Inn*, accompanies the 1964 publication of the book. Its final paragraph contains a rather puzzling mention of the Revolution in the East – most likely the Soviet Union and communism – and urges the younger generations to learn about the past while saluting "the present transformations" brought about by the working class. Most likely, the note was inserted into the text to placate communist censorship.

12. Two famous mountain tops in the eastern range of the Carpathians.

13. The word *Moș*, followed by a man's name, is a polite form of address in the rural areas of Romania, the equivalent of "Old Man" in English-speaking communities.

14. The unification of Wallachia (home province of the shepherd from Vrancea) and Moldovia in 1859 ended with national unification in 1918 when Transylvania (home to the Ungurean shepherd) was reunited with the other Romanian provinces in the aftermath of WWI.

15. For a summary of the *Miorița*'s plot, see Chapter 2, "(De)Gendering the *Miorița* Ballad: Mihail Sadoveanu's *The Hatchet*." For an excellent critical commentary of the ballad, its history and cultural background, as well as an exquisite English translation complete with beautiful pictures illustrating the ballad's lines, see Ernest H. Latham in *Miorița: An Icon of Romanian Culture* (Iași: The Center for Romanian Studies, 1999).

16. Benedict Anderson, *Imagined Communities. Reflections on the Origins and Spread of Nationalism* (London: Verso and New Left Books, 1983).

17. Regis Debray, "Marxism and the National Question," *New Left Review*, 105, (Sept.- Oct. 1977), 26-27.

18. Roman is today a small town in northeastern Moldavia, but at the turn of the nineteenth century it was a flourishing center where people from all over Moldavia gathered to attend seasonal fairs. Centuries earlier, during the reign of Stephen the Great and Holy (1457-1504), Roman had been a fortified, well-guarded fortress that had resisted the Tartars' and the Turks' frequent attacks against Moldavia.

## *The Disheveled Maidens* of Bucharest:
## A New Moral and Fashionable Geography of the City

Focusing almost exclusively on women characters, Hortensia Papadat-Bengescu's 1926 novel *The Disheveled Maidens*[1] addresses significant 1920s Romanian cultural, moral, and social concerns. A distinct set of anxieties, developed in reaction to the country's moribund nineteenth-century landowning and agricultural culture and in direct response to the moral geography of the increasingly urbanized space of Bucharest, Romania's capital, is presented through the gendered lenses of a young female narrator named Mini.

Since, as Eli Zaretsky (1997) argues, the gender distinction that lies "at the heart of nineteenth-century culture" allied the values of "mastery, self-control or reason" with men, and those of "passivity, dependence and emotionality" with women, any disruption in the gender-social order of the early twentieth century lay in a breakdown of self-control or virtue necessarily coded as feminine.[2] And since cities seemed to be the source and space of women's worst vices, sexual indulgence and over-consumption, in Papadat-Bengescu's *The Disheveled Maidens* women who give in to their sexual passions and who move away from traditional environments to embrace city life become agents of social change in the city's fashionable new moral and urban geography.

I have argued elsewhere that in general Romanian women's voices have been silenced or marginalized as a result of the country's cultural patriarchy.[3] Of course, a minority of women of upper- and middle-class households did manage to contribute to the public sphere, especially in the urban milieu and literary circles. The cultural activism and literary works of Papadat-Bengescu, for example, remain a remarkable legacy of early twentieth-century Romania where the socio-economic conditions and educational structures combined to disempower women. Engaging in the discourse of defining women's new identity and their role within a still patriarchal cultural space, Papadat-Bengescu's *The Disheveled Maidens* makes room for Mini, the author's mouthpiece, whose first-name-only identity suggests that her identification by a full name is less important than her reporting on events while maintaining a sharp-eyed focus on the city and its inhabitants. Her role is (1) to uncover the growing participation and inclusion of women in the moral geography of the Romanian nation and its capital; and (2) to detect and record the extent to which the potential disordering of the country's traditional society corresponded to the emergence of a changing type of femininity engaged in redefining women's roles in modernity.

As narrator-observer, Mini relates the disintegration of Lenora and Doru Hallipa's marriage (a metaphorical allusion to the collapse of the old order) and their subsequent move to the city; as urban commentator lured by the magic of Bucharest, the city she loves, Mini chronicles the living city with its streets, intra-city transport, public buildings, private residences, museums, shops, and the multitude of inhabitants. In this regard, Mini's review of Bucharest's well-known landmarks is not unlike the lengthy city descriptions in Theodore Dreiser's *Sister Carrie* (1900), a novel which details the location and nature of Chicago's and New York's theatres, restaurants, hotels, and major streets and to which *The Disheveled Maidens* bears more than a casual resemblance.[4]

The intersections of Mini's complex narratorial functions provide ample occasion for the portrayal of the socially constructed and morally meaningful female types of the time. From the sexually indulgent Lenora Hallipa, through her promiscuous daughter Mika-Lé and Mini's feminist friend Nory, to kind-hearted Doctor Lina and the fashionable Elena Hallipa, to the alienated, nameless women of Bucharest, all the feminine characters bear in some form or another the unmistakable trademarks of the disheveled maidens of the title who find their haven in the city.

Out of step with the Romanian cultural assumption of the era, which required that young girls or unmarried women in the outskirts of the city – as well as in towns, villages, or even more rural places – wear their hair braided and tight on their head (*împletite*) as a sign of their virginity, the new, fashionable women of *The Disheveled Maidens* appear in public with their hair loose, dyed blonde, wild, or curly (*despletite*). Thus although no mention of tightly-braided hair pertains to the heroines of *The Disheveled Maidens*, and even though through the course of events they do become spiritually disheveled or distraught, the novel's title in Romanian, *Fecioarele despletite*, which I have translated as *The Disheveled Maidens*, serves as an outright sign that Papadat-Bengescu's heroines, having long lost their virginity, purity, and innocence, have ceased to adhere to traditional cultural norms.[5]

The association of a woman's unbraided hair with sexual depravity appears early on in the novel when Mini speaks of a woman who had just given birth to a baby, born as if from her blond, snake-like curls:

> I saw a young girl, wearing a yellow silken shirt under her hospital gown, bending over a little yellow worm of a baby she was holding in her lap. A huge wave of curly blond hair hung spread over her face; through the golden snakes of this adornment, I could hardly make out a withered, ugly face. Surely, that poor yellowish larva had been born from that amazing hair. (46)

Unlike the novel's disheveled maidens, especially her feminist and radical friend Nory who wears her hair "cropped short on the nape" (63) and makes gender-specific comments and never misses a chance to promote her socialist views, Mini is an extreme figure, a feminine character who transgresses gender norms. She flourishes in the city's spaces and suffers whenever she is away, as in the first scene of the novel, when she is accompanying her woman-doctor friend, Lina, to the Hallipas' mansion in Prundeni, two and a half hours by carriage from Bucharest. Worried that she might have to spend the night in the country, Mini is an unwilling witness to the crisis of the Hallipas' deteriorating marriage which is manifested in Lenora Hallipa's mood swings, particularly her "passionate, selfish, noisy and whimsical conjugal love" (4). In one such scene, for example, as her husband takes her hands, Lenora "pulled them free with a jerk, started crying, and then finally embraced him amidst huge sobs, but as soon as he hugged her, she pushed him away and fainted again, causing a little panic" (14).

As Lenora alternates moments of total abandon to her husband's affection with scenes of great anxiety when she inexplicably seems to hold him accountable for her recurrent and seemingly senseless misery, it soon becomes clear that the current crisis has to do with the latest exploits of their strange-looking, dwarfish daughter Mika-Lé. Different in appearance from the other Hallipa children – the beautiful Elena, who, like Mika-Lé, still lives at the Hallipas' aristocratic mansion in Prundeni, another daughter Coca-Aimée, and twin boys who are studying abroad – Mika-Lé is the daughter with a sordid past. Having been expelled from her classes at Notre Dame for her sexual involvement with a seminarian, Mika-Lé has now deliberately triggered – because of her immodest relations with a neighboring estate owner, Prince Maxențiu – the breakup of her elder sister's Elena's engagement to the Prince.

After throwing Mika-Lé out of their home, the Hallipas are, however, unable to return to normalcy. To assist with Lenora's frequent breakdowns and general depression, her cousin Lina, a practicing women's doctor, makes daily trips to the Hallipas' estate from the neighboring capital Bucharest, where she lives with her husband, Doctor Rim. Lina is one of the few intimates in Lenora's circle who knows that Mika-Lé is not Doru Hallipa's daughter, but rather the product of a brief affair Lenora once had with an Italian painter brought to decorate an addition to the Hallipa residence. Unaware that Mika-Lé is not his daughter and thus unable to fathom the depth of Lenora's despair at the wretched girl's behavior, Hallipa tries in vain to bring the good old days back. With Elena's marriage to the *nouveau riche* Drăgănescu and her move to Bucharest, and with Mika-Lé giving birth to a stillborn child of uncertain paternity, Lenora grows increasingly despondent and must leave the Prundeni estate to seek treatment in a sanatorium. Under the excellent care of Doctor Walter, Lenora recovers and makes a full and public confession of Mike-Lé's illegitimate birth, thus derailing the young woman's plan to extort money from Doru Hallipa.

Although the Hallipa story is the novel's putative plot, there is less care to the characterization of the principal characters in *The Disheveled Maidens* than to the reporting of the events through Mini's eyes. Mini's connection to the Hallipas, as well as to the other characters in the book, is fragmented and has little to do with creating or sustaining their personal relationships. Although the circumstances that *The Disheveled Maidens'* plot offers are, conventionally, among the most dramatically exploitable in literature – Mika-Lé's scribbled note to Hallipa asking for money after she had been thrown out of the house, the break-up of Elena Hallipa's engagement to Prince Maxențiu and her subsequent wedding to the wealthy Drăgănescu, or the final collapse of the central relationship of the book marked by the Hallipas' divorce and the selling of the Prundeni estate – Papadat-Bengescu disdains the dramatic opportunity in each instance. No direct confrontations, with their inherent possibilities of conversational drama, take place between her characters. Instead, they reveal their feelings through Mini's narrative account in ways that express the lack of necessity for dialogue.

The clue to the significance of this pattern lies, on an immediate level, in the fact that characters resemble puppets moved by strings of sexual desire and what moves the plot in each episode is sexual impulse.[6] Lenora Hallipa, for instance, who "had gained precocious knowledge of all aspects of life" (76), discovers early on the sexual power she has over men. Having had her share of sexual encounters, as well as a first husband, from a large supply of military officers stationed in her native provincial town of Mizil, she then marries young Doru Hallipa, the sole heir of a sizeable fortune complete with a family estate. As the new mistress of the beautiful mansion, Lenora is "a haughty nymph lustily sprawl[ed] on the bed of her conjugal love" (8).

Although she lacks her mother's beauty, Mika-Lé, the girl who has "the head and complexion of a faun" (9) and "eyes like bogs that wouldn't drip" (118), gains a shameful reputation in her early youth. She then moves into artists' circles and becomes involved in scandalous sexual liaisons that are the talk of Bucharest. In *The Disheveled Maidens*, no less than in all her other writings, Papadat-Bengescu seems determined to show that sex should be recognized as the controlling and directing force that it is. Sexuality, firm and insistent in its pressure, is what ultimately gets communicated from the inarticulateness of Lenora, as she clings to Doru's arms and lips. Between bouts of hysterical self-indulgence, Lenora fits admirably Spencer's description of a fairie, with "hair disheveled, wringing hands and making piteous moans."[7]

Pounding in manifold guises against the walls of the Hallipas' existence, sexual impulse is all that propels their actions and ultimately expresses their identities. Substantiating this conceptualization, the novel forwards an obsession with the corporeal, body parts or even hair that signals the body as symbolic of the characters' identity and as a register of gender anxiety. When the Hallipas' household is in turmoil during her first visit at Prundeni, Mini introduces Lenora as

> the beautiful Mrs. Hallipa, the lady of the house.... Her complexion as of a blonde puppet, a Nuremberg puppet with a small red mouth and pink porcelain-like cheeks, was tensed up and the large

blue eyes, those eyes of limpid glass, were red with weeping. The regular waves in her bleached hair, as golden as a wig, were now distorted; her majestic, plump body, always aware of its generous stature, was now lying languidly, exhausted, carelessly wrapped up in a morning gown. (2)

In similar ways throughout the narrative, Lenora's erotic posturing, "her puppet-like figure, round, white, pink, made-up and smiling" (17), makes the character appear dehumanized in her fragmentation into body parts, not a whole. Mini, who is unable to visualize Lenora "wearing street garments, far from a bed with a tulle canopy and mauve ribbons" (72), talks about "her neck, where the veins stood tense under the fat white flesh" (3); her "white, muscular arms waving around in the air" (8); her "white velvety hands" (2); or her rosy lips chewing on her morning cigarette, a habit that makes Lenora look even more seductive.

Complementing her sensuous body, Lenora's dyed-blonde hair functions as a decorative cultural signifier, adapted to embody both the character's social function and her upper-class status. It is an outward projection of the Prundeni mistress's successful rise from her humble beginnings in the small town of Mizil to the social ideal of feminine beauty in 1920s Romania.

The key to Lenora's (im)morality is her body – a "bulk of passive flesh" governed by "her primitive feelings, uncontrolled by her small intelligence" (75). Mastered by passion, not reason, Lenora gives in to her own passions that lead her to sexual overindulgence and push her to commit the most serious of moral crimes – adultery. Her seduction by the Italian painter, an encounter that leaves Lenora pregnant with Mika-Lé and that still seems to reverberate with the silent and lascivious echoes haunting the deserted hallways of the Prundeni mansion, ultimately causes the collapse of the Hallipas' old world.

Registering another dimension of Lenora's insatiable sexuality, Mika-Lé is an even more disturbing sexual addict than her mother. According to Mini's feminist friend Nory, Mika-Lé's exemplars are Boccaccio and Casanova, whose infamous practices and sexual perversions she masters early on. Having turned the Hallipas' household into a citadel of pain more than once, Mika-Lé stands as a warning against sexual depravity and its monstrous consequences. Born from violent desire, she is "the tiny boil grown on the spot of the violation" (57), the ulcer that mocks the "natural" cooperation of reproduction between a man and a woman.

Like Lenora, Mika-Lé is also shown mostly in a fragmented way. Her "broad teeth on broad jaws…[and] square wooden shoulders" (25) and her "wild, curly, African-like hair that grew straight up" (9) make her resemble "a wooden country puppet" (25). To Mini, Mika-Lé conjures up unpleasant and insect-like imagery – "her head like a black mosquito, her immobile eyes, those two ovals of yellow liquid, and her skinny body like that of a rickety child" (25).

Like the novel's women, men also appear to be activated by sexual impulses only, from the barely sketched Lică, the Troubadour, "slim, sprightly teasing the girls of the neighborhood over the fences with a little stick" (83), to Doru Hallipa, a sexual puppet whose "bondage was absolute" (8). Passionate about his horses and a first-class rider "who pulls hard at the reins" (13), Hallipa had submitted to "the life of perpetual love [that] forbade him friends" (5). During Lenora's crises, when he is reduced to a "tormented, hen-pecked" (101) husband by his voluptuous wife, Hallipa's goggling eyes, tousled hair, poorly trimmed beard and half-crazy look point to his physical degradation and progressive dehumanization.

On the heels of his divorce from Lenora, Hallipa is back in high sexual gear in his pursuit of Eliza, the fiancée he had abandoned after being seduced by the experienced Lenora in his youth. Caught unaware by the rapid pace of Hallipa's sexual advances, Mini, who meets the visibly changed former owner of the Prundeni estate and his new conquest at the museum, notices Eliza's "tenderness [that] involves precursory traits of voluptuousness" (140) and Hallipa's meticulous elegance, his well-polished fingernails, elegant town clothes, and "his beard cut much shorter and very carefully trimmed" (141). After the brief and unexpected meeting with Mini, the two depart, "Hallipa, with the gait of a hunter tired by the chase, taking his prey to his den. Eliza, clinging on to Doru's arm, dragging her narrow shoes, look[ing] like a swamp duck in the damp air; a panting, hot, sheepish game" (142).

Further substantiating its demonstrable eroticism that actively transgresses characterization, *The Disheveled Maidens* displays a deep sensitivity to the spatiality of desire. The very shapes of rooms and spaces in the Hallipas' mansion are invested with a libidinal charge. What appears to be more commanding and thrilling than the plot is erotic power, an oblique possession in which jouissance is derived from a moment of erotic tension that is scenically conceived.[8] Thus even though the Italian painter that once seduced Lenora is just a dimly-perceived, long-gone figure who no longer achieves sexual possession of Lenora's body, he does still take oblique possession of a space that is infused with erotically charged power and that is still capable of subjecting Lenora to its own libidinal force. Ultimately, oblique possession involves an eroticism that thrives on the dissolution of the sexes, male and female, into the scene of jouissance that makes it not only impossible but also unnecessary to picture the lovers' individual identities clearly. What is left is a veritable spatialization of desire in which spatial elements, like the painted ceiling in the Hallipas' mansion, constitute a crucial relay in the libidinal circuit that is set up – "an absurd ceiling like a summer sky, with cotton-like balloons of white clouds against a jarring blue, probably the work of the Italian, the man who had passed that way. In that decor you could imagine them all playing an absurd pantomime, with broken gestures" (28-29).

A realm comprised of erotic spaces, the Hallipas' Prundeni mansion offers to its puppets, Lenora and Doru, the experiences they crave in the overall spatial effect of its "peaceful yet sensitive body" (13). From the very beginning, from the architecturally erotically inscribed gate to the estate, which indirectly announces the possessive pathway Doru takes each time he enters the mansion to gain access to Lenora's voluptuously draped body, to Lenora's "white, pink and mauve alcove, full of lace and ribbons in amorous and naïve colors, with angels on the ceiling and roses on the walls" (21), there is a strongly suggested sense of promiscuity. And although as a whole the Prundeni mansion manages to be a space of inordinately untempered monotony, as a conjugal domain it bears a corporeal or phallic dimension captured in the sense of things: "the grandfather clock with gentle shades" (1); "the limpid voice of the bronze tongue [of the clock] striking another quarter" and "the bronze chords in the large ebony piano" (11); and above all the unfinished vestibule. Done years ago according to Lenora's taste and, unbeknownst to Hallipa, the site of her illicit affair with the Italian painter hired to complete the artistic portion of the project, this room is now deserted by all except Mika-Lé, "a contemporary to the new addition [who] has a bias for it and [who] used to play here when she was little and even now" (30). In her lonely strolls through the Hallipas' mansion Mini, who sarcastically calls the vestibule "the Shakespearean setting of the tragedy" (28), notices

the gradual shade of the naked, smooth, round columns, left in the visible plaster stone...that Hallipa's hieratic complexion, the tortured, Medusa-like head on Lenora's goddess-like body.... The same unpolished, sandy mosaic on the floor resembled a paved desert in which you could imagine your steps melt down noiselessly. Then the chalky white of the walls up to mid- height, and, above, the foolish paintings: the Pompeian frames and the panels with nymphs and angels, the same nymphs that poorly resembled Lenora and the same plump angels. (28-29)

This space of desire, like others in *The Disheveled Maidens,* is one in which contingent desire has not been organized metaphorically, definitionally into sexuality. Rather, the characters' imprint takes oblique possession of the spaces, a possession that does not involve physical penetration of the space, but does amount to a metaphoric penetration of the space's overall character.

The erotic potential that governs in such spaces of desire is complemented by the individual attraction that exists between Lenora and Doru. At the time of the crisis in the Hallipas' household, the erotic tension between husband and wife is enriched due to the obliquely libidinal economy that is enacted in their relationship. Thus Lenora's anguish whenever her husband is away and her annoyance with his presence is a dynamic complemented by Doru Hallipa's perverse attraction to Lenora, his arousal fueled by the power of refusal that she may wield toward him. Compounding the issue, Lenora's determined attempts to push her husband into Eliza's arms, for instance, result in Hallipa's agonizing efforts to stay loyal to his wife in what comes across as a twisted enactment of conjugal love to Mini, the reluctant observer:

> In one form or another Lenora kept trying to get Doru involved with Eliza; the obvious intention was that he be as obliging as possible to his cousin. "You've hurt Eliza…"; "Give Eliza a hand…"; "Why don't you tell Eliza?"; "You'd better sit on the other side, by Eliza!" … Innocent and full of grace, Eliza was letting herself be spoiled, while she went on waiting on her. As Doru was impatient to leave Lenora by herself in Lina's company, Mini did him this good turn by expressing her desire to see the deserted foyer. As if moved by some dramatic event, Lenora shouted, "But how can you leave Eliza behind?" With a grimace of annoyance and a hardly controlled nervous gesture of both his hands, biting his lips, Doru waited for the clumsy, high-heeled Eliza to descend the three asphalt steps of the terrace and, floating on the blue heels of her tiny shoes, join them. (108)

Doru Hallipa's conjugal claim to possess Lenora by trying to put up with her erratic behavior and irrational demands creates the very conditions that will allow her to bring the crisis to an end. Indeed, her decision to confess Mika-Lé's illegitimate paternity, which puzzles

Cousin Lina, is not so hard to grasp once we realize that the very decisiveness with which Doru tries to bind her to himself endows Lenora with the energy to set off on a different path. This process is most strikingly brought out in the erotic power of the moment reported by Nory, a witness to the entire scene. As Doru, the recipient of every bit of Lenora's discontent, tries to protect Lenora from Mika-Lé,

> Mika-Lé threw herself to Lenora's feet asking for forgiveness and for…money. It seems she'd been told about the undoing of the Hallipa estate. Blue in the face and not knowing what to do, frightened at what might have happened, Doru dashed at the little bug, but Lenora stopped him.
>
> "She is quite right addressing me," she said, "because it's only I who has the right to deal with her." And she confessed the secret of Mika-Lé's birth…in what terms…I do not know…. Very calmly and clearly, says Lina, who was unable to recover her wits. And as everybody present was petrified and had lost the faculty of speech, Lenora, the most cold-blooded in the gathering, advised Mika-Lé, as a fortuneless mother, to work harder than she had so far and earn her living. (135)

It is as if sex, no matter how twisted, were almost the only imaginable form of personal interchange in Papadat-Bengescu's world since all other contacts have been reduced to the account other characters give of their interactions. Nevertheless, sex in *The Disheveled Maidens* does not enrich relationships beyond what they initially were. Sex is merely the instrument of a compulsion to have a relationship, or a marriage, a compulsion excited by a whole complex of inarticulate assumptions about the representative glamour of a particular person. At the end of what in most novels would be very complicated human attachments, Papadat-Bengescu's characters simply walk off, stumbling into other sexual liaisons and acquiring new identities in what the narrator repeatedly calls "the living City." In the sequel to *The Disheveled Maidens* and the second novel of the Hallipa trilogy, *A Bach Concert*, all the protagonists live in Bucharest, where Lenora is married to Doctor Walter and Doru Hallipa to Eliza.

This curious, very sad, and touching episode, showing that nothing has been gleaned from the tangled emotional and social relationships that hold people and families together, points to the need for a refiguration of sexuality via femininity in modern times. In this context, Walter Benjamin's view of woman as an allegory of modernity, as the ruin of the traditional auratic woman, the object of man's desire exploited as a mechanism of aesthetic perception, opens up the emergence of a new feminine presence, whose altered perception allows her to survive in the alien environment of the city. Here young women like Mika-Lé, who in the morally rigid system of the country did not conform to the dictates of respectability, become exemplars of the increasingly urbanized crowd that differed dramatically from the family-oriented culture that had characterized Romania to that point. Unlike another socially constructed female of the time, the prostitute who exhibits her sexuality, the loose woman of Mika-Lé's type is loose only from the bounds of a moralized space, like that of the traditional world of the Hallipas where Lenora's "bizarre case of moral adultery" (27) singles out and penalizes the potentially traumatic consequences of casual sex.

Created out of a related but distinct set of social anxieties and associated therefore with a different moral geography of the city, these new women, the disheveled maidens, align their own sexually-charged images with the environment of the modern city. Overcoming a prostitute's hard luck and fate with their own elevated function of sexuality as more than merely the satisfaction of a drive, they attach to it a value of hallucination. Sexuality seems to be something else for these disheveled maidens who enjoy their freedom, their individuality, and their power to live out their wishful fantasies by investing the city with libidinal energy. Seeking their own fulfillment, they reveal their own intoxicating desire and experiences that one might well take to be the modern equivalent of aesthetic experience. And in the process of giving in to their whims, they represent an intersection of time and place where the experience of the city can no longer be distinguished from a sense of being. As they "shed the burdens of their sins by hurriedly giving birth to sons fathered by absinth or punch" (61) here, in the city, the disheveled maidens become addicted to fashion, which is born from their repressed libidinal desires and which corresponds to their need of novelty.

Like the women of Western cities, the disheveled maidens of Bucharest also bear the anxieties connected with mass consumer culture, mainly because they belonged in the major class of consumers as the group whose identity was focused on outward appearance. And

since Bucharest was the economic capital of Romania, it was also the
first place in which mass culture and consumerism were made manifest
in the landscape by what the morally upright called "desiring" women.[9]

Combining desire and fashion to create the new appearance of
femininity, these desiring women with very narrow hips and wearing
the latest fashions appear to Mini as models bearing the professional
perfection of the mannequin. Ushering in the new age, they emerge as
ideal support for fashion – "scrawny mannequins [with] dull skin, ex-
aggeratedly large eyes, and lanky, scraggy hands; on their narrow busts,
[they have] breasts whose vain attempts at showing off were more sala-
cious than any voluptuous forms" (86). Fashion provides such disheveled maidens with a surface image behind which their bodies disappear
reducing them to an image predicated on the aesthetic appearance once
supplied by traditional art. Substantiating Luce Irigaray's statement,
"the moment the look dominates, the body loses its materiality,"[10] the
disheveled maiden who fascinates Mini has a dead, or anorganic,
body,[11] a thing which fashion can disguise:

> She used to walk around in ball gowns of a nakedness that induced
> no trace of impudence in the aspect of her absent body, and this
> could deceive customers, while in the fiery tuft of her hair she dis-
> played the insolent glory of an immense egret. Or she would dis-
> appear in the rigid circumference of hoop-skirted flounces, in
> some stylish model, her forehead tightly bound with some broad
> ribbon, which made her head look quite morbid. (61)

In the city, fashion as disguise and commodified desire as pleasure
project the new appearance of femininity, as well as the implicit illusion of bliss and faded promiscuity that recommend the disheveled
maiden:

> She was a regular nightly customer of restaurants frequented by
> foreigners, in which drinking, not love making, was the main vice,
> and she was reputed for her prim attire and her everlasting insom-
> nia. Night after night she kept staring at the yellowish liquid in the
> permanently filled glasses! ... Who knows what caprice of alcohol
> or betrayal of sleep had once dishonored the artifice of her barren
> orgies.... (61)

As modern allegory, the disheveled maiden is an enigmatic figure, in whose commodified body the feminine aura that once surrounded woman is destroyed. Still, the exhibition of a dead body in the corpse of commodity must be faked by disguise and make-up to cover up its commodity and use value that make her appear as

> something between a puppet and a woman; with thick eyeliner on her eyelashes and eyelids so that her eyes looked like two black spots on their chalk-white face; her hair, short at the nape, while at the front she wore it as a curly tousle, violently peroxided and so high that it exceeded the tiny, wrinkled face. (61)

This commodity character, who has created a new principle for life in modernity and whose allegorical figure is woman as commodity, is also known as a "painted" woman; she is the demimonde who inhabits city spaces representing a particularly potent and obvious form of transgressive behavior, a specific type of (im)morality.[12] Since her attractiveness is based on the skill with which she disguises her real looks, either through makeup or stylish clothes, she uses fashion to hide her true self. Related to sexual passion but also suppressing it, her fashion sense or her passion for clothes and dry goods, her idleness, boredom and vanity lead her down the perilous path of over-consumption.

The disheveled maidens of the city are thus everything a traditional woman was not supposed to be. This is why, I think, there is so much anxiety expressed around Lenora's or Mika-Lé's giving in to their twisted sexuality or around the painted woman's fascination with outward appearance and dress. Both types of indulgence not only upset the precarious balance between self-control and self-indulgence, but also lead to societal changes. Morality could not be mapped so easily in the big city where the emerging spaces of consumerism did not distinguish between ladies and painted women, respectable citizens and charlatans, those who were good and those who were evil:

> In the simultaneous game of transformations you couldn't tell whether they were born from literature or were the very models from which extreme literature was born. Baudelaire and Verlaine, two classicists when you read them now, were circulating in thousands of human forms and the decadent man was the normal

everyday man, at whom their older brothers still looked in
amazement, and who could hardly wait to become a classic in his
turn and to be replaced.

Under tortuous appearances, simple souls were taking pains to
lead complicated lives, while dubious characters lived under old
and honest firms. What lunacy! (87)

Thus, although Mini's focus tends to sidestep immoral behavior,
she has to acknowledge from Nory's reports respectable houses that
hide upstairs brothels and respectable girls who are prostitutes in the
living city. While informing Mini of Mika-Lé's whereabouts, for example, Nory speaks of the young girl's new quarters in Autumn Street:

"A lot of doors open into the so-called refectory of this honorable
boarding house. Two long tables covered with oilcloths and vases
holding paper flowers, both pushed to the wall; a ruin of a piano, a
large iron stove; a merry and cheap life…. True enough, they do
eat poorly, but the boys come up with supplements…. Do you
know, Mini, that the boss in Autumn Street is the divorced wife of
A., the master of the Bar Association? She is worn out. She is ugly
and 'evil,' as Lina would say. She patronizes at the head of the
table with her 'fancy man,' her pimp, at her right side. The little
rooms on the    *entresol* and the garret are for 'youngsters;' they let
them now on credit, now on installments. On the first story she has
rooms fit for couples 'just passing through' or eloping. It is the
specialty of the house. They get separate room service…. In the
afternoons the bosses retire to play poker arranged around thiev-
ery. They skinned the son of Vrana, a millionaire; the boy was
underage and rather stupid. Lică, too, calls there at times and has
his share" (117).

Assembled from Mini's inner thoughts and commentaries, the
novel's abundant city imagery and her perception of the strange characters going their way in the city provide vignettes not so much of isolation as of an alienated environment that allows the subjects to survive
by meaningfully relating to the scenery of urban energy. Mini's own
experiences in the city and her perceptions felt not as an experience of
the other but as a perception of the same everywhere create a way of
guarding herself against the threat of dissolution. Imagining the city as
a belt, Mini "felt it there, around her. A belt so close and so precious

that it seemed to be made of the very fibers that sustain the diffuse substances of our own body within our structure, which by its consistence girdles the fluid dispersion of our blood" (85).

Papadat-Bengescu's choice of a feminine narrator as the woman embedded in the city is probably no coincidence. According to Aaron Betsky, "we often personify cities as women, which are seen as realms of femininity as opposed to the masculinity of nature. In fact, one of the recurrent themes in Western history, from the Song of Songs to the stories of the Moors in Spain, is that of the rulers who conquer or build a city who is then feminized by the women living in it" (32).[13] Betsky's point is certainly echoed in *Sister Carrie*, where the heroine manages to create a powerful space for herself as another person who is the very embodiment of the city. Her ability to buy into and re-create the realm to which women are assigned and through which they define themselves enables her to make her way in the city, first Chicago and then New York. By the end of the book she has become an actress, in complete control of her destiny in and through the city that is her stage.

Although Mini's trajectory is in many ways different from Carrie's, she too is the embodiment of a modern woman who manages to create a powerful space for herself in the city through which she reaffirms her femininity. Much of *The Disheveled Maidens* focuses on Mini who becomes part of the spectacle of the city by roaming its indeterminate space and by continually observing and reporting the changing composition of forms, colors and textures into which all inhabitants are dissolving.

Mini's response to Bucharest too can be illuminated in the light of oblique possession. The city, which she sees as "noble, vast, luminous," a force that "called you and absorbed you in its power, giving you a feeling of healthy, tender joy" (48), is Mini's own space of desire. Here she feels "her heart throbbing" and her lips wet with the drizzling rain "wetting them like juice" (144). Even when she finds herself at night in parts of the city that she does not know very well and which she can barely make out through the shroud of evening frost, Mini is "afraid as of something that couldn't really hurt, while the place, even if unknown, was, nevertheless, familiar, as though, with closed eyes, she'd been in well-known arms" (58).

The streets, the streetcars, everything that manages to produce this obliquely possessive sense is the very towswoman space, with all the energy that its intense, both confusing and exciting activities generate. Thanks to her traveling through the city – a zone of veritable quicksand, a magical land, free of interaction between individual persons, so fascinating and so arresting – Mini is able to associate herself contiguously with it, to take in the sense of the breathless scenes with their staccato rhythm.

A sprightly figure within the magical city, with "her heart pounding hard as if she had been handling the huge chain and the key of the sacred citadel" (61), Mini surrenders to the urban experience through a relaxation of her ego's defenses. Transposed, she unconditionally accepts and embraces the city's apparitions: "the madmen, different yet related by their exaltation…all of them decidedly showing one common trait: they were all starved, of bread, of meat, of people, of life. Hungry! Their insanity was that of hunger" (46). Filled with an all-consuming desire to rush forward and embrace her beloved city and "the immense multitude of people" (61), Mini joins with the countless throng and becomes a part of the great current of city life.

In final analysis, the time and space of *The Disheveled Maidens* is, by comparison to what allotted to personal relations, inordinately devoted to Mini's reporting of the city of Bucharest, the great living city that she loves. And with less care given to the characterization than to the characters' environment and their move to the city, Papadat-Bengescu spares no effort in highlighting the Romanian capital in the interwar period –Bucharest's golden age. Much enlarged by the peace treaties at the end of World War I, Romania, and especially Bucharest, became a Mecca for European and American travelers. Writers and journalists like Emil Hoppe, John McCulloch, Paul Morand, James T. Shotwell and John Reed, the American war correspondent who found Bucharest "sunk in luxury and sloth,"[14] spent time in the capital, as did the famous Countess Waldeck, the *Times* correspondent.

In her book *Athene Palace,* Waldeck wrote extensively about Bucharest as a city "irresistibly between East and West, between ancient and modern, between rustic and metropolitan…[where] people came because it was the terminal of all traffic between Europe and the Orient, and a stop here was necessary on the way to and from more or less mysterious missions" (257).[15] Her descriptions of the city turn into photograph-like images, like the ones capturing winter in Bucharest when "a thick fur of white padded everything, lying in luscious cushions on the cupolas of the hundred-odd Byzantine churches"; or of the Bucharestians who "exposed themselves to the temptations of the Calea Victoriei – the latest Paris perfumes, English woolens, Viennese leather goods, and mountains of salami, candies, and *marron glacés*...and lingered in the *Cartea Românească*, the Brentano's of Bucharest, where you could get books in every language" (258-9).

Written a little over a decade earlier than Countess Waldeck's book, *The Disheveled Maidens* is also a chronicle of Bucharest's golden days, "an admirable epoch..., in which there were samples of all generations moving about" (87). While featuring many of the places mentioned in *Athene Palace*, Papadat-Bengescu's narrative of the city and its people uses Mini's love of Bucharest, which she personifies, to portray a new world, where men and women mixed, where "women...could have walked about smoothly and majestically in a peplum [even] when there were so many forms of transition towards a plastic pattern of the future" (87), and where all people could construct their own identities. Substantiating Papadat-Bengescu's own view that "towns...possess a power of their own which fights and conquers all the laws of nature" (32), the characters of *The Disheveled Maidens* live in an ever-changing realm, full of possibilities, where

> the numerous Pleiades of intellectuals ravaged by the violent out-
> burst of the war [WWI] were carved into reduction by the new diet
> and the new morality. They were the ones who didn't make up a
> nation, but represented it on all occasions where aspect was the
> essential requirement; those of the first rank placed in the first row
> at all spectacles. Yet...the ones seated behind them were exactly
> those that comprised the reserve forces, the most important ones,
> the surprise and the resources of production, the commissioning of
> the latest moral and anatomical novelty (87).

In the rapid rise to prominence of new groups of people in the city, Elena Hallipa's husband, Drăgănescu, who is mentioned by his last name only, stands for the increasingly urbanized and industrialized class of Bucharestians, not only in the scale and pace of economic development and change, but also in the values and mores of the varied socio-economic classes newly created. With money becoming the predominant measure of all value in society, Drăgănescu's family pro-gresses from its modest beginnings as innkeepers to an ever-expanding class of *nouveau riche* – a journey marked by the trajectory from Old Mother Tar, Drăgănescu's mother who "used to tar the old stale barrels [to store the family's wine] from a tar pot" (65), to Drăgănescu's rise as vice-president of the Chamber of Commerce and venture capitalist. His marriage to Elena Hallipa, a daughter from the class of the landed gentry, and their elegant home on one of Bucharest's most fashionable streets, Lascăr Catargiu, confirm the old adage of the solidity and stability of land being progressively undermined by the culture of money.

Duplicating Drăgănescu's "*noblesse de baril,*" which is what Mini calls Drăgănescu's recent social elevation, is the ambitious flour magnate, the *parvenu* Ada Razu. One of the most snobbish girls in the fashionable dancing halls, this "queen of flour" (59) marries the feeble Prince Maxenţiu, the landowner from Plăieşele who was once engaged to Elena Hallipa. The Prince, who moves to the city after selling his land, follows the same pattern as Doru Hallipa, the agent of patriarchal tradition and "rustic feudal lord," who sells the Prundeni country estate and becomes transformed by the town and the present times "into a poor bourgeois, bringing only the cloth of a tent he might pitch on the edge of the town with him" (124-5). In the incredible fluidity of Bucharest's socio-economic system, both Hallipa and Prince Maxenţiu stay "a component in decomposition...scattered around the living city as separate individuals, pieces severed from a decomposed whole, for each of them to become an initial spring of new activity" (142). Addressing indirectly the acute concern about pressures on landed culture and its fading role in the culture of the nation, the two landlords' move to the city makes clear that the biggest threat to landed culture at the dawn of modernity is the culture of money.

Adding to the number of those whom Mini receives into her living city – Lenora, Lică, Lina, Elena, Mika-Lé, Doctor Rim, and even Mini herself – Hallipa and the Prince illustrate the massive shift from the rural world to the urban milieu in 1920s and 1930s Romania. In one of her many moments dedicated to admiring the city, Mini observes the increasingly crowded capital, "people walking, people behind walls, these or others.... Inhabitants of the living city, coming from all parts, naturalized there for one reason or another.... Unknown, with their indifferent personal stories, as well as those with well-known stories.... These or their fellow humans, enveloped in the rain" (116).

For all newcomers, as for Mini, the city is "a haven…the Promised Land" to which they come "to conquer life where its pulse had the richest beat" (43). Itself a space of desire, Bucharest is the fertile ground where distinct new species could be identified, where order and the virtues developed in the country continued to fall apart, and where morality was questioned – "the slum girl had disappeared or become exotic, and the new plebeian professions, typewriting and manicure, had changed the face of the slums. The taxi driver was the quintessence of the slum boy, coached through mechanics as through fire, to assume the select form which yesterday still used to lead to 'anything' " (87).

Granted, Bucharest is not New York, Romania is not America, but they were something, and in Papadat-Bengescu's *The Disheveled Maidens* Bucharest is an all-consuming and magnetic capital that somehow suggests the Western capitals, complete with its assortment of houses of ill-repute and street apparitions, like the one Mini sees often

> wear[ing] a long riding coat with nothing underneath in the middle of winter and a pot hat; he had a black beard and held an old leather briefcase in his hand; he had a serious, wise air, was walking calmly, with equal steps, chasing women along the same way, between Alcalay and Socec, uttering a sort of prayer, which, at its end, begged in ecclesiastical terms, "charity for love." A hungry beggar that gave you a strange fear by this participation of God in the insanity of the world. (47)

Having traversed the space of almost six centuries from its first mention as a mere residence on the Danubian plain recorded in 1459 by the Wallachian ruler Vlad Țepeș,[16] the Romanian capital is complete with the gravity of smooth, tall, imposing edifices that lined up perfectly and with its inhabitants coming from all parts of the country:

> The passers-by were numerous, and they were trying to squeeze between those people on the Central Canal of the city, that stretch of confluence between the Palace and the boulevard. They stopped for a moment at the corner of the Elisée to prepare for their crossing. The National Theatre was standing there in its tiny square; old, but still preserving some grandeur. Like two affluent streams, one illuminated, the other obscure, Câmpineanu and Matei Millo

Street flowed down by its sides, providing a little waving on the
plain of Bucur's grazing field. (62-3)

As she looks through the translucent fog toward the novel's end,
Mini embraces the town that she loves. Earlier on, in the rain, she had
"compared her soul to that of Master Manole's wife" who, immured
alive in the walls of the church built by her husband, becomes one with
his creation.[17] Like Ana, the Master's wife who hurries through the
flood and the rain to reach the church with the food she is taking to her
husband, Mini projects herself in an emerging metaphor of identification with the city, her master toward whom she is forever rushing "with
her brave little feet…hurrying ahead relentlessly…soaked in the
streams…undefeated in the yearning to arrive carrying in her little
hands the food of the master, protected and kept warm by the heat of
her palms" (127).

Mini's love of and focus on Bucharest, the living city, is a potent
indication of the importance of the capital in the critical decades of the
1920s and 1930s both in terms of economic growth of the city and of
the expansion of its structural form. To the architect-designed ornate
office and government buildings, the city experienced the construction
of two types of public places: those that served to display its cultural
status (theaters, museums, parks) and those that served consumer
demands (stores, restaurants, dance halls). Mentioned in Mini's
description of the city, the National Theatre and the Museum of Art, as
well as the Capşa and the Nestor restaurants and coffee shops, were
landmarks inscribed into Bucharest. Like New York or Chicago in
*Sister Carrie*, Bucharest, the capital, becomes for modern Romania
"part of the hieroglyph of the race"[18] – the space of a network of public
spaces within the city that were characterized by the activities of consumption and the display of social status. Of particular interest for my
point here is that a good deal of these spaces were open to, in fact
catered to, women – women defined first and foremost by the fact that
they were Bucharestians flourishing in the city's public spaces.

Among these women Mini is a powerful presence. Encoded in the cityscape, she offers an alternative cultural panorama of modern Romania, one that does not shut out the old order but reframes it as a set of vignettes. Her gentle and detailed observations encompass the domestic code of country life dissipated from within to make room for unions like the marriage of Elena Hallipa (the old gentry) and Drăgănescu (capitalist entrepreneur); and, with a surplus of visual imagery, the rise of urban life, energized by its disregard of a stable, ordained order and by the release of a destructive extemporizing energy, such as Mika-Lé's.

Carefully controlled through Mini's defused perspective and the novel's use of little direct speech, *The Disheveled Maidens* presents a new society that subtly reformulates gender roles. It offers a different model of manliness – domestically submissive to women, sexually controlled, and socially inept – and it inscribes a new sphere for women where they substitute aesthetic experience with an experience of illusion by manipulating their appearance to their advantage. Both elevated and contained as fashionable figures or endlessly false appearances, Lenora the "haughty nymph," Nory the feminist, Cousin Lina the doctor, the snobbish Elena Hallipa Drăgănescu, the social climber Ada Razu Maxenţiu, and the sexually *outré* Mika-Lé, are just a few of the disheveled maidens, the new and fashionable types of femininity that help articulate the nation's modern identity.

### *Notes*

1. *The Disheveled Maidens* is the first of a trilogy that includes the novels *A Bach Concert* (1927) and *The Hidden Road* (1928). All were read in installments, as they were being written by Papadat-Bengescu, during the literary soirées of the literary *cénacle* Sburătorul.

2. Eli Zaretsky, "Bisexuality, Capitalism and the Ambivalent Legacy of Psychoanalysis," *New Left Review* 223 (1997), 69-89.

3. Ileana Orlich, *Silent Bodies: (Re)Discovering the Women of Romanian Short Fiction* (Boulder and New York: East European Monographs/Columbia University Press, 2003).

4. Written only two decades apart, *The Disheveled Maidens* and *Sister Carrie* also share two strikingly evident paradoxes: a solid, self-conscious attempt to anchor their narrative in early twentieth-century Romanian and American life, which ultimately succeeds in foregrounding their modernity; and the power and endurance of both novels, in spite of what critics at large have often considered to be an awkward and inept prose style.

5. My translation of the title in English, *The Disheveled Maidens,* takes into account the Middle English "disheveled," from Old French *deschevele,* past participle of *descheveler,* to disarrange the hair: des – apart; dis + chevel (hair, from the Latin *capillus).* "Disheveled," according to *Webster's Unabridged Dictionary* (New York: Random House, 1996) is "1. Having in loose disorder; disarranged; as disheveled hair. 2. Having the hair in loose disorder." "The dancing maidens are disheveled Maenads" – J. A. Symonds.

6. This belief is generally embraced by most Romanian critics who follow the respected George Călinescu's view that Papadat-Bengescu's writings are "an essentially feminine literature, with no exit from the close circuit of the sexual condition.... The life of the senses...with implicit confidence in these values, are the only aspects with which she deals extensively. What a woman feels physically when she is in good health or taken ill, how she wants or repudiates a man...these are the writer's themes." *History of Romanian Literature,* translated by Leon Levițchi (Milan: UNESCO NAGARD Publishers, 1988), 627.

7. These lines from Edmund Spencer's *Faerie Queene,* Book Two, stanza 13, lines 6-7, describe Duessa, a female villain who, disguised as a raped woman, is trying to trap the male hero of Book Two into fighting the male hero of Book One, the Redcrosse Knight.

8. I use here Gert Buelens definition in the excellent essay "Henry James's Oblique Possession: Plottings of Desire and Mastery in *The American Scene,*" *PMLA* 116 2 (March 2001): 300-13.

9. See K. Peiss, "Making Up and Making Over: Cosmetics, Consumer Culture, and Women's Identity," in *The Sex of Things: Gender and Consumption in Historical Perspective,* ed. V. de Grazia (Berkeley, CA: University of California Press), 311-36.

10. Cited by Craig Owens, "The Discourse of Others: Feminists and Postmodernism," *The Anti-Aesthetic: Essays on Postmodern Culture,* ed. Hal Foster (Port Townsend: Bay Press, 1983), 70.

11. See, for example, Luce Irigaray again, as quoted by Alice Jardine, "Theories of the Feminine: Kristeva," *Enclitic* 4, No. 2 (Fall 1980): 5-15.

12. For a detailed discussion of this term, see Karen Halttunen, *Confidence Men and Painted Women: A Study of Middle-class Culture in America, 1830-1870* (New Haven: Yale University Press, 1982).

13. Aaron Betsky, *Building Sex: Men, Women, Architecture, and the Construction of Sexuality* (New York: William Morrow and Company, Inc., 1995).

14. Reed, who made Bucharest his headquarters for ventures into the war zones in neighboring Serbia, Russia, Bulgaria and Turkey, made the infamous comment in a letter sent to his friend and former professor Charles Copeland.

15. Rosa Goldsmith, a.k.a. Countess Waldeck, first published *Athene Palace* in 1942 (New York: Robert M. McBride & Co). The book received excellent critical attention. *The Christian Science Monitor* (May 29, 1942) called it "a spicy record of observations made in one of the world's most volatile of social and diplomatic populations" (p. 12). Recently, *Athene Palace* (Iasi: The Center for Romanian Studies, 1998) was published in Romania, with excellent notes, comments and introduction by Ernest H. Latham, Jr.

16. The legend says that Bucharest was founded by a shepherd named Bucur; another variant, more likely, is that it was established by Mircea cel Bătrân in the fourteenth century after a victory over the Turks (*bucurie* means joy in Romanian, which is why Bucharest is often called "The City of Joy"). Bucharest is first mentioned under its current name as a residence during the reign of Vlad Țepeș (Vlad the Impaler) in a 1459 court

document. It soon became the summer residence of the court. In 1595 it was burned by the Turks; but, after its restoration, it continued to grow in size and prosperity. In 1698 Prince Constantin Brâncoveanu chose it for his capital. After the unification of the Romanian provinces Wallachia and Moldavia in 1859, Bucharest became the capital of the Romanian state declared in 1861. In the second half of the nineteenth century, the population of the city increased dramatically. The extravagant architecture and cosmopolitan high culture of this period won Bucharest the nickname of Paris of the East (or little Paris), with Calea Victoriei as its *Champs Elysée.*

17. The folk ballad *Master Builder Manole*, has critically been interpreted as "a portrait of the artist forced to sacrifice the woman he loves for the sake of his art." For a different point of view in the interpretation of this enduring literary masterpiece of Romanian folk tradition, see the chapter "Master Builder Manole" in *Silent Bodies.*

18. I am indebted to Richard Poirier, who uses this formulation in "Panoramic Environment and the Anonymity of the Self," Theodore Dreiser, *Sister Carrie,* ed. Donald Pizer, Norton Critical Edition (New York: Norton, 1970): 583.

# The Authors

## Ion Agârbiceanu
## (1882-1963)

Considered a master of the "moral" short-story, Ion Agârbiceanu was born in Agârbiciu, a small Transylvanian village. As a clergyman, Agârbiceanu was preoccupied with the permanent struggle between the temptations of life and Christian virtues, and his prose style in general, as seen in *Fefeleaga*, approximates sermonizing. Among his notable works, are the short stories *Datoria* (The Duty), *Legea trupului* (The Law of the Body) and *Legea minţii* (The Law of the Mind). As the titles suggest, all these stories focus on moral righteousness and Christian values, that, as another short story titled *Biruinţa* (The Triumph) proclaims, must always vanquish the evil. Although these stories explore human conscience and its constant moral battles with sin, their narratives are linear, with no moral complications.

Given Agârbiceanu's rather predictable style and narrative range, the novel *Sectarii* (The Sectarians), which depicts the political scene of post-WWII Transylvanian society, is a surprising work. Filled with unexpected wit, the novel focuses on a journalist protagonist, Ilare Zopârlan (the last name is an approximation of "low-class" in Romanian), a character with no moral restraint who offers humorous reports on political manners and claims to high-culture assumed by Romania's post-war *nouveau riches*.

Agârbiceanu's masterpiece is undoubtedly the story *Fefeleaga*, the only work among the vast number of his narratives to be anthologized often.

## Mihail Sadoveanu
## (1880-1961)

Toward the end of his life, Mihail Sadoveanu enjoyed the satisfaction of seeing his books sell out, be included in school textbooks, and become instant classics. Very few Romanians would not have read his celebrated *Baltagul* (The Hatchet), which is a fictionalized version of the traditional ballad *Miorița* (The Ewe Lamb) or *Viața lui Ștefan cel Mare* (The Life of Stephen the Great).

Sadoveanu's extraordinary popularity, which only a small group of writers enjoyed in the former Eastern European bloc countries, stems from his talent as well as his deep attachment to the history, culture, and traditions of the Romanian people. During his life Sadoveanu published over one hundred books. Among them are the well-known novels *Frații Jderi* (The Brothers Jderi), *Neamul Șoimăreștilor* (The Șoimaru Family) *Hanu-Ancuței* (Tales from Ancuța's Inn), and *Venea o moară pe Siret* (A Mill Came Down the Siret). Sadoveanu also wrote a number of novellas, including *Nunta Domniței Ruxandra* (The Wedding of Princess Ruxandra), *Cazul Eugeniței Costea* (The Case of Eugenița Costea) and *Haia Sanis* (1909), which the respected literary critic George Călinescu considered to be the writer's most balanced work from a dramatic point of view.

During the last years of his life Sadoveanu enjoyed tremendous recognition and was actively engaged on the sociopolitical scene both in writers' circles and, politically, in the People's National Assembly, where he served as one of its delegates.

## Ioan Slavici
## (1848- 1925)

The son of the master furrier Savu Slavici and his wife Elena, Ioan Slavici was born in Şiria, near Arad, in the western part of Romania. After leaving his native village early on to attend school in Arad, Timişoara and Pesta (Hungary), he enlisted in the army of the Austro-Hungarian Empire. An important moment of his life occurred in 1871 when he met and befriended the greatest Romanian poet, Mihail Eminescu, in Vienna before embarking on the most prolific decade of his literary career. After the completion of military school in Vienna, Slavici became an officer in 1871.

Slavici's literary debut is marked by the publication of *Fata de birău* (The Innkeeper's Daughter) in 1871. The following year, after leaving Vienna and starting a law practice in Arad, he published the stories *Zâna Zorilor* (The Dawn Fairy), *Ileana cea şireată* (Shrewd Ileana) and *Floriţa din codru* (Floriţa of the Woods).

In 1874, Slavici moved for a short period to Iaşi, the cultural center of Moldova, in eastern Romania, where he became the editor of the newspaper *Curierul* (The Dispatcher). A year later he moved to Bucharest and worked for the newspaper *Timpul* (Time). During this time, he published one of his early masterpieces, *Popa Tanda* (1875) and a collection of short stories, *Nuvele din Popor* (Stories of the People, 1881).

In 1882 Slavici became a member of the Romanian Academy, traveled to Italy and accepted a teaching appointment at the Elena Doamna School in Bucharest where he taught Romanian and Philosophy. In 1884 he moved to Sibiu, a central city in Transylvania, as editor of the literary journal *Tribuna*, a position which enabled him to introduce to the public the young poet George Coşbuc. He continued to publish other stories, such the novella *Pădureanca* (The Woman of the Woods, 1884), and the historical drama *Caspar Graţiani*. After marrying Eleonora Tănăsescu in 1886, he was elected Secretary of the Romanian National Party and, in 1888, was jailed for a year in Vaţ, Hungary, for relentlessly advocating the interests of the Romanian community in Transylvania.

Deeply saddened by Eminescu's untimely death in 1889, Slavici returned to Bucharest and began in 1890 his four-year tenure as a

Professor at the Elena Doamna School. In 1894, together with Coşbuc and the playwright Ion Luca Caragiale, Slavici became a founding member of the literary magazine *Vatra* (The Hearth), where he published his recently completed novel *Mara*.

Slavici published another volume of short stories, *Nuvele* (Novellas) in 1896 and a first volume of *Poveşti* (Stories) in 1908. At the peak of his recognition as a writer, Slavici became a member of the Romanian Writers Society, which was created in 1909.

During the last years of his life which were spent in relative obscurity, Slavici published personal narratives with a confessional character that reflected his own life: *Închisorile mele* (My Prisons, 1921), *Scrisori adresate unor prieteni din altă lume* (Letters to Friends from Another Realm, 1921), and *Lumea prin care am trecut* (The World in Which I Lived, 1924). Before his death in 1925, Slavici published his last two novels, *Ultimul Armaş* (The Last Armash, 1923) and *Din păcat in păcat* (From Sin to Sin, 1925).

Slavici's enduring reputation rests on such famous short stories as *The Lucky Mill* (1881) and the novel *Mara*, his masterpiece.

## Hortensia Papadat-Bengescu
## (1876-1955)

The daughter of a general and his teacher wife, Hortensia Papadat was born in Iveşti, a rural community north of the town of Galaţi, in southern Moldavia. At the age of twenty she married an attorney, Nicolae Papadat, and spent the first years of her marriage following him to the various locations his job assignments took the young couple. After giving birth to several children, she published her first work, *Ape adânci* (Deep Waters) in 1919. Highly praised by such leading literary critics of the period as Garabet Ibrăileanu, this early novel resulted from Papadat-Bengescu's association with the literary coterie *Viaţa Românească.*

During World War I she volunteered as a railroad station nurse in Focşani, an experience she evoked in her 1923 novel *Balaurul* (The Dragon). Following the war years she joined the literary group *Sburătorul,* whose members initially dismissed Papadat-Bengescu's early work as both awkward and facile. Under the mentorship of Eugen Lovinescu, one of *Sburătorul's* respected leaders, Papadat-Bengescu eventually turned from what was perceived as her dilettante style toward the "objective" prose that she developed in the Hallipa cycle, *Fecioarele Despletite* (The Disheveled Maidens, 1926), *Concert din muzică de Bach* (A Bach Concert, 1927), and *Drumul Ascuns* (The Hidden Road, 1928). In 1933 Papadat-Bengescu moved to Bucharest where she completed the novel *Logodnicul* (The Fiancé) in 1935 and *Rădăcini* (Roots) in 1938. In 1946 she was awarded the National Prize for fiction.

Literary critics are divided in the evaluation of Papadat-Bengescu's work. For Eugen Lovinescu, Papadat-Bengescu's novels continue the Proustian tradition and set the tone of urban fiction in Romanian literature. Discussing her work in *A History of Romanian Literature*, detractors like George Călinescu consider her prose "flat" and decree that the author's "entire work is a long, refined gossip of a woman of the world, in an impossibly spoken language" (p. 627). In Călinescu's views, which have influenced Papadat-Bengescu's reception among post-WWII Romanian readers, the feminine characters of her novels are the most inadequate, as they "visit each other and gossip, giving birth to the literature of bedroom secrets, of scandals and scandalous innuendoes."

Largely forgotten by the general public and ignored by those writers favored by Romania's communist regime, Papadat-Bengescu lived the last years of her life in poverty. At her death, in 1955, the critic Constantin Ciopraga spoke for many of the novelist's dedicated readers when he stated that she was "on the Via Magna of the Romanian novel."

# Works Cited

Agârbiceanu, Ion. *Fefeleaga. Russian and Eastern European Literature.* Ed. James Miller Jr., Robert O'Neal, Helen M. McDonnell. Glenview, IL: Scott, Foreman, and Co., 1970.

Anderson, Benedict. *Imagined Communities. Reflections on the Origins and Spread of Nationalism.* London: Verso and New Left Books, 1983.

Barthes, Roland. "Drame, poème, roman." *Sollers écrivain.* Paris: Edition du Seuil, 1979. 11-45.

Benhabib, Seyla. "The Generalized and Concrete Other: Toward a Feminist Critique of Substitutionalist Universalism." *Praxis International* 5, No. 4. (1986): 402-424.

Benjamin, Walter. "The Work of Art in the Age of Mechanical Reproduction." *Illuminations.* Ed. Hannah Arendt; trans. Harry Zonh. New York: Schoken Books, 1968.

Betsky, Aaron. *Building Sex: Men, Women, Architecture, and the Construction of Sexuality.* New York: William Morrow and Company, 1995.

Blaga, Lucian. *Trilogia culturii.* Bucureşti: Editura pentru Literatură Universală, 1969.

Buelens, Gert. "Henry James's Oblique Possession: Plottings of Desire and Mastery in *The American Scene.*" *PMLA* 116, No. 2 (March 2001): 300-13.

Călinescu, George. *History of Romanian Literature.* Trans. Leon Leviţchi. Milan: UNESCO NAGARD Publishers, 1988.

Corniş-Pope, Marcel. "Literary and Cultural Production in a Marginocentric Cultural Node: The Case of Timişoara." *A History of the Literary Cultures of East-Central Europe: Conjunctions and Disjunctions in the 19th and 20th Century.* New York, Amsterdam: John Benjamin Press, 2003/2004.

Debray, Regis. "Marxism and the National Question." *New Left Review* 105 (Sept.-Oct., 1977): 26-27.

Derrida, Jacques. *Of Grammatology.* Baltimore: Johns Hopkins University Press, 1976.

Dostoyevsky, Fyodor. *Crime and Punishment.* Trans. David McDuff. Harmondsworth, Middlesex, England: Viking, 1991.

Eagleton, Terry. "The Marxist Rabbi: Walter Benjamin." *The Ideology of the Aesthetic.* Oxford: Blackwell, 1990. 316-40.

Eliade, Mircea. *The Fate of Romanian Culture.* Trans. Bogdan Stefanescu. Bucureşti: Editura Athena, 1995.

Genette, Gérard. "Frontiers of Narrative." *Figures of Literary Discourse.* Trans. Alan Sheridan. New York: Columbia University Press, 1982.

Georgescu, Vlad. *The Romanians: A History*. Ed. Matei Călinescu; trans. Alexandra Bley-Vroman. Columbus: Ohio State Press, 1991.

Halttunen, Karen. *Confidence Men and Painted Women: A Study of Middle-class Culture in America, 1830-1870*. New Haven: Yale University Press, 1982.

Hennessy, Cecily. "Iconic Images of Children in the Church of St. Demetrios, Thessaloniki." *Icon and Word: The Power of Images in Byzantium*. Ed. Antony Eastmond and Liz James. Burlington: Ashgate Publishing, 2003. 157-173.

Hyde, Lewis. *The Gift: The Imagination and the Erotic Life of Property*. New York: Vintage, 1979.

Jardine, Alice. "Theories of the Feminine: Kristeva." *Enclitic* 4:20 (Fall 1980): 5-15.

Jackson, Robert Louis, ed. "Philosophical Pro and Contra in Part One of *Crime and Punishment*." *Twentieth Century Interpretations of "Crime and Punishment*. Englewood Cliffs, NJ: Prentice-Hall, 1974.

Kayser, Wolfgang Johannes. *The Grotesque in Art and Literature*. Trans. Ulrich Weisstein. Gloucester, MA: P. Smith, 1968.

Kristeva, Julia. "Le temps des femmes." *Cahiers de recherche de sciences des textes et documents* 33/34, no. 5 (Winter 1979); trans. Alice Jardine and Harry Blake, "Women's Time." *Signs* 7:I (Autumn 1981): 15.

Latham, Ernest H. *Miorița: An Icon of Romanian Culture*. Iași: The Center for Romanian Studies, 1999.

Nemoianu, Virgil. "Biedermeier Cultural Intertextuality in Transylvania: The Case of Ioan Slavici." *The Comparatist: Journal of the Southern Comparative Association* XVI (1992): 62-69.

_____. "Learning over Class: The Case of the Central European Ethos." *Cultural Participation: Trends since the Middle Ages*. Ed. Ann Rigney and Douwe Fokkema. Amsterdam: John Benjamin Press, 1993. 79-107.

Newman, Victor. *Tentația lui homo-europaeus: Geneza spiritului modern in Europa centrală și de sud-est*. București: Editura Științifică, 1991.

Orlich, Ileana Alexandra. *Silent Bodies: (Re)Discovering the Women of Romanian Short Fiction*. Boulder and New York: East European Monographs/Columbia University Press, 2002.

_____. *Ioan Slavici*, Mara, *Translation and Critical Commentary*. București: The Romanian Cultural Foundation Publishing House, 2003.

_____. *Mihail Sadoveanu*, Tales from Ancuța's Inn: *Translation and Critical Commentary*. București: Editura Institutului Cultural Român, 2004.

Owens, Craig. "The Discourse of Others: Feminists and Postmodernism." *The Anti-Aesthetic: Essays on Postmodern Culture*. Ed. Hal Foster. Port Townsend: Bay Press, 1983.

Ortner, Sherry B. "Is Female to Male as Nature is to Culture." *Woman, Culture and Society*. Ed. Michelle Zimbalist Rosaldo and Louise Lamphere. Stanford: Stanford University Press, 1974.

Peiss, K. "Making Up and Making Over: Cosmetics, Consumer Culture, and Women's Identity." *The Sex of Things: Gender and Consumption in Historical Perspective*. Ed. V. de Grazia. Berkeley: University of California Press, 1996. 311-36.

Piru, Alexandru. *Istoria Literaturii Române*. Bucureşti: Editura Grai şi Suflet – Cultura Naţională, 1994.

Poirier, Richard. "Panoramic Environment and the Anonymity of the Self." *Theodore Dreiser, Sister Carrie Norton Critical Edition*. Ed. Donald Pizer. New York: Norton, 1970.

Rauch, A. "The Traverspiel of the Prostituted Body, or Woman as Allegory of Modernity." *Cultural Critique* 10: 77-88.

Ricoeur, Paul. *Oneself as Another*. Trans. Kathleen Blamey. Chicago: The University of Chicago Press, 1992.

Sadoveanu, Mihail. "The Hatchet. *Classics of Romanian Literature*, Vol. III. Trans. Eugenia Farca. Boulder and New York: East European Monographs/ Columbia University Press, 1991.

Sandel, Michael. *Liberalism and the Limits of Justice*. Cambridge: Cambridge University Press, 1982.

Sedgwick, Eve Kosofsky. *Between Men: English Literature and Male Homosocial Desire*. New York: Columbia University Press, 1985.

Spenser, Edmund. *The Faerie Queene*. London: Dent; New York: Dutton, 1966.

Stone, Lawrence. *The Family, Sex and Marriage in England 1500-1800*. New York: Harper and Row, 1977.

Vârgolici, Teodor. "Postfaţa la *Hanu Ancuţei*." Bucureşti: Editura 100+1 GRAMAR. (2001) 117-122.

Zaretsky, Eli. "Bisexuality, Capitalism and the Ambivalent Legacy of Psychoanalysis." *New Left Review* 223 (1997): 69-89.